Kevin Hancock

Advance Praise for *The Seventh Power*

"Kevin Hancock's personal journey holds universal messages for people at all levels of business and community. *The Seventh Power*'s new, more inclusive approach to leadership and management will give you important insights into your life, your career, and your company."

—CHIP CONLEY, Hospitality Entrepreneur and Bestselling Author

"In his latest book, *The Seventh Power*, business visionary Kevin Hancock lays out a practical plan for how to make businesses more profitable and healthy, so that everyone—customers, owners, and employees—all flourish. I highly recommend this groundbreaking book."

—CHRISTIANE NORTHRUP, MD, *New York Times* bestselling author of *Women's Bodies, Women's Wisdom*, and *Goddesses Never Age*

"Many business books have discussed management, innovation, culture, and how to be great, but none grab you like Kevin Hancock's *The Seventh Power: One CEO's Journey Into the Business of Shared Leadership*. One has to admire what Kevin has accomplished after acquiring a rare voice disorder. Kevin takes what to most of us would be an insurmountable challenge and uses it as a learning tool to make himself, those around him, and his company better. *The Seventh Power* is not only a good read, it's a must read for all aspiring leaders and even those of us who have been around a while. It's never too late to learn!"

—RICK HOLLEY, Chairman of the Board, Weyerhaeuser Company

"I have always admired Kevin for the reputation he has among the folks working for his organization. The leadership skills and management style described in this book are inspirational, transformational, and motivating. I am thankful that Kevin is generous and willing to share his perspectives on a fresh path to corporate excellence through employee centric thinking."

—GEORGE EMMERSON, President, CEO Sierra Pacific Industries

"Powerful. Genuine. Transformative. Those three words sum up the wisdom and humanity that Kevin shares in *The Seventh Power*. By focusing on the intrinsic value of individuals, his vision and examples of shared leadership from organizations worldwide make this the rare leadership book that effectively transcends and challenges the traditional top-down management model. If you're looking for a fresh, authentic take on how a company can power up its people, its value to society, and its performance, you've found it."

—RICK SCHUMACHER, *LBM Journal*

"From his home in Maine to Navajo and Lakota communities in the West to Ukraine, Kevin Hancock takes the reader on a personal journey of more than 15,000 miles in which he learns to listen and empower people. The Seventh Power is an exploration of a new model of leadership in which individual voices are heard and the human spirit is celebrated. The principles that Kevin puts to work in his 171-year-old family business offer an enlightened way forward for all institutions."

—SUSAN COLLINS, *U.S. Senator*

THE SEVENTH
POWER

THE SEVENTH
POWER

ONE CEO'S JOURNEY
INTO THE BUSINESS OF
SHARED LEADERSHIP

KEVIN HANCOCK

PRESS

A POST HILL PRESS BOOK

The Seventh Power:
One CEO's Journey Into the Business of Shared Leadership
© 2020 by Kevin Hancock
All Rights Reserved

ISBN: 978-1-64293-406-9
ISBN (eBook): 978-1-64293-407-6

Cover art by Jomel Cequina
Interior design and composition by Greg Johnson, Textbook Perfect

Post Hill Press
New York • Nashville
posthillpress.com

Published in the United States of America

This book is dedicated to my dad,
who was asked to lead his whole life—start to finish…
and
to the victims and survivors of the Holodomor.

AUTHOR'S NOTE

This book is related to, but not dependent upon, my first book, *Not for Sale: Finding Center in the Land of Crazy Horse*, which chronicled my first six trips to the Pine Ridge Indian Reservation from 2012 to 2014, and my initial search to recover my voice after being diagnosed with a rare neurological speaking disorder called spasmodic dysphonia (SD). That book was about healing through spiritual awakening. I was trying to regain my authentic voice, and so, too, were the people of Pine Ridge. The parallels between their story and mine were unlikely yet numerous.

This book picks up in 2017, and it's about integration. Seven years after acquiring SD, and five years after first traveling to Pine Ridge, I paused to examine what I had learned from those experiences and how I incorporated (or might still better incorporate) that learning into my work as the President and Chief Executive Officer of one of America's oldest companies.

In this story, I set out on a new series of travel adventures designed to test, refine, and validate one formative idea: organizations are most effective when the opportunity and responsibility for leading is shared broadly and embraced by all. Power, it turns out, is meant to be dispersed.

The mission was to take this knowledge and transform a personal awakening into a corporate renaissance.

* * *

THE AMERICAN MYTHOLOGIST JOSEPH CAMPBELL identified three phases to the universal human experience of loss as a harbinger for growth. First comes the moment of *initiation*, in which an unanticipated event destabilizes the world as we know it. It is here that a loss occurs. This time of crisis calls forth a period of *separation*, in which the featured character travels to a strange new land in the hope of recapturing that which has been taken away. At the conclusion of this odyssey, the seeker often discovers an unexpected boon of riches. This bounty is often symbolized as a treasure chest filled with gold, but in essence, the prize is a fresh set of eyes with which to view the world.

Finally, the hero arrives at the most difficult task, which Campbell called *the return*. The central figure of the story is now compelled to return home and impart the gift of insight that he or she has acquired. This is the pattern by which humanity advances. All learning is individual before it becomes collective, and loss is a prerequisite for gain.

According to Campbell, the Hero's Journey has "a thousand faces," because it is a path that all of humanity is invited to walk. We are all heroes, and that shared leadership adventure is central to this story. If my first book was about initiation and separation, this one is about the return.

In the end, we always go home....

* * *

IN THE STORY THAT FOLLOWS, I travel over 15,000 miles, from my hometown in Casco, Maine, to a remote Indian charter school on the edge of the Colorado Plateau, and eventually all the way to

Kiev, Ukraine. The unexpected journey was a puzzle filled with clues about the nature of "power" and how it might be used more carefully and shared more broadly. Along the way I encounter a collection of inspiring individuals and exceptional communities that are transforming the traditional framework of leadership, followership, and organizational excellence. These encounters ultimately blossom into a series of insights as to how CEOs and other leaders might elegantly break down the planet's entrenched, top-down governance model in favor of a new playbook for heightened human engagement, hallmarked by shared leadership, dispersed power, and respect for all voices.

Having found a piece of my own authentic voice, I wanted to help others do the same, and a lumber company in Maine became an unlikely platform where this could occur.

* * *

MY THREE FAVORITE THINGS to share are a smile, a hug, and an idea. Each, once exchanged, becomes forevermore collectively owned. Everyone's learning belongs to us all, because all of life is connected by a web of invisible strings. *In that spirit, it takes a writer and a reader to give a book true life—so thank you.*

In closing, anyone writing a book about life and leadership should begin by confessing how little they know, how often they have erred, and how human they are.

—*Kevin Hancock*

The True Peace

The first peace, which is most important, is that which comes within the souls of people when they realize their relationship, their oneness, with the Universe and all its powers, and when they realize that at the center of the Universe dwells Wakan Tanka (the Great Spirit), and that this center is really everywhere—it is within each of us. This is the real peace, and the others are but reflections of this.

The second peace is that which is made between two individuals, and the third is that which is made between two nations.

But above all, you should understand that there can never be peace between nations until there is known that true peace, which, as I have often said, is within the souls of men.

—BLACK ELK

CONTENTS

INTRODUCTION

The Presence of a Seventh Power

"All birds, even those of the same species, are not alike, and it is the same with animals and with human beings. The reason Wakan Tanka does not make two birds, or animals, or human beings exactly alike is because each is placed here by Wakan Tanka to be an independent individual and to rely upon itself."

—SHOOTER, LAKOTA SIOUX

In the spring of 2013 I visited the Pine Ridge Indian Reservation for the second time. On that trip, I had the opportunity to learn from a spiritual circle of young people who were strengthening their community through a return to core Lakota values.

One young man, wise beyond his years, was discussing the symbols of his culture when he paused and picked up a porcupine-quilled medicine wheel that lay on the table before us. "The medicine wheel represents the Six Great Powers," he said, referring to the sky, the earth, and the four cardinal directions.

"These powers are all extensions of the Great Spirit, Wakan Tanka, who is everywhere and present in all things. The sacred energy of the Universe does not just surround us; it is also within us."

While this understanding—that every individual is sacred—is prevalent in many indigenous cultures, it is rarely incorporated into the leadership philosophy of modern human organizations. Why? What established rules of governance might be threatened? Conversely, what new approaches to excellence might be achieved with the knowledge that every individual holds a piece of the Great Spirit within?

"Here, at the center of the medicine wheel, some who know the old ways say that a Seventh Power also exists," the young man continued.

"What is the Seventh Power?" I asked, sensing that something important was coming.

"The Seventh Power is you. The Seventh Power is me. The Seventh Power represents the individual human spirit," he explained. "Each of us is a gift of the Great Spirit. Every person's thoughts and actions change the world."

A community in which authentic self-expression had been systematically oppressed for generations was rebuilding itself from within, one soul at a time, through the recognition of a Seventh Power that dwells within us all.

* * *

We all adhere to a belief system. Otherwise we don't have a strategy for dealing with the world.

—JOSE MIGUEL SOKOLOFF

"LET'S START AT THE END," Colombian-born advertising executive Jose Miguel Sokoloff once told me. We were enjoying an English breakfast in the Burlington Gardens section of London, where Jose was about to describe how Christmas trees and soccer balls helped to end more than fifty years of guerrilla warfare in his native land.

In Jose's honor, let's start at the end of this story...

It's a Wednesday evening in early May. More than a thousand people are dressed to the nines at Pier Sixty in New York City as the sun sets across the Hudson River on the twenty-fifth anniversary gala of the internationally renowned Seeds of Peace Camp. The organization was founded in the summer of 1993, when forty-six teenagers from Israel and Palestine were coaxed into spending three weeks together in a row of rustic cabins on a quiet lake in Maine.

The mission of Seeds of Peace is to cross a seemingly unbridgeable divide and bring peace to the Middle East—one teenager at a time. Twenty-five years after its founding, the camp has more than 6,700 alumni scattered around the blue planet we all call home. I grew up across the lake from the camp, and that connection is what brings me here.

To our left, at the center of the long hall, Mandy Gonzalez—currently starring in the Broadway show *Hamilton*—is leading a diverse group of green-shirted teenagers through a spirited rendition of Sara Bareilles's hit song "Brave."

Say what you want to say
And let the words fall out

Shortly thereafter, former vice president Joe Biden takes the stage.

"Any conflict is nothing more than a loss of personal relationship," Mr. Biden says.

His words remind me of the wisdom of Thomas Walker Jr., a Navajo peacemaker, who shared this with me nearly one year ago: "First, we must understand that we are related to every person and creature we see. Then, we must honor our responsibilities to those relationships."

"All around the world, young people are seizing their power," Mr. Biden is saying. "For the beauty that lives within us all to fully blossom, the narrative of 'It's the other person's fault' must first be overcome. We change that mind-set by looking first within ourselves."

Biden is speaking in a soft tone about a big idea. The true path to deep social change does not reside in a capital or rest in the hand of an iconic chief executive. It lives dispersed, inside us all.

* * *

FOR CENTURIES, SOCIETIES ACROSS THE GLOBE have been systematically indoctrinated into the belief system that power, control, and higher authority live "out there" somewhere, beyond our reach, in a faraway capital, with a government leader, a distant God, or a controlling executive. Empires, you see, have most frequently amassed power by convincing individuals to cede some of their own. In the bureaucracies and hierarchies that followed, a few at the center came to speak for the many. Individuals, in turn, were trained to place the needs of headquarters or capitals above their own. The needs of the capital come first. The individual is taught to sacrifice and serve.

But the Lakota understanding of a Seventh Power represents a fresh path, born from ancient wisdom, in which a country, community, or company can be made strong, one person at a time. If every individual is free to follow their own voice, the community as a whole can thrive.

Around the planet, enthusiasm for, and engagement in, traditional institutions is waning. Only 33 percent of Americans will describe themselves as being "engaged" in their work and a mere 17 percent believe they can trust their government to do what's right. The effectiveness of all five of the planet's big social institutions—family, school, place of worship, place of work, and government—is all being impaired.

What's driving this institutional malaise? It's the twenty-first century awakening of the Seventh Power and its corresponding awareness that individual aspirations are not forever destined to be sacrificed on behalf of the empire. An organization-centric world order long designed to serve kings, clerics, and chief executives is now being called upon to yield to a new social template focused on creating value for individuals and dispersing power instead of centralizing it.

But change comes hard, and the established institutional governance model is deeply entrenched. While humans are increasingly looking for communities where the individual is featured and honored, most organizations still remain self-absorbed. The result is a planetary organizational slump defined by low levels of human engagement and marginal effectiveness.

* * *

THIS BOOK IS ABOUT THE POTENTIAL for unleashing an unprecedented wave of organizational excellence through the recognition and embrace of the Seventh Power. I'm not simply talking about valuing employees or caring for constituents; the importance of that is already broadly understood. I'm talking about something fundamentally different, which is the celebration of the individual for his or her own sake, beyond one's ability to contribute to the company or community economically. This new vision views the company or institution as an incubator, an accelerator, and a servant of each employee's individual human quest for growth. There is no substitute for self-esteem and self-worth in the creation of a healthy society. Work can become the primary endeavor by which adults self-actualize and grow stronger. When individuals grow stronger, the world around them changes for the better. Helping people find their voice and tap the power that dwells within them can change the world.

Since the onset of the agricultural revolution, human organizations have been hierarchical and bureaucratic. Laborers were commodities. For thousands of years, nation-states were not much different. The population was expected to serve the empire first and foremost. Individuals were overtly and covertly taught to take pride in their expendability.

But deep change is coming. Society, long structured to put the empire first, is becoming individual-centric. This does not mean that the end of collaboration and cooperation is upon us; it simply means that the ground rules for organizational excellence must be reinvented to fit the age in which we live.

In the old corporate model, for example, the employees existed to serve the company. In the new model, the company exists to serve the employees. When this happens, corporate performance actually improves, but as an outcome of a higher calling. When leaders of established organizations answer this universal call for authentic self-expression, they bend the curve of social evolution toward a more dynamic and collaborative future for all. I believe this is our human destiny. Honoring and leveraging the power of the individual spirit is the new path to dynamic group performance.

And while any institution can make this change, businesses—agile and localized by nature—are uniquely positioned to improve the world by honoring the voices of others.

The sacred energy of the Universe is dispersed. It lives within us all. Strengthening a sense of power in others is the true calling of a great leader and can become the new mission of free enterprise. A tribe is made strong one individual at a time.

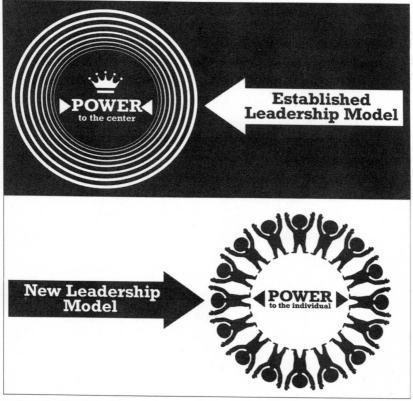

Organizational excellence in the twenty-first century will require a new script. Leadership responsibility is destined to be dispersed, not collected.

It is extremely hard to discover the truth when you are ruling the world. You are just far too busy. Most political chiefs and business moguls are forever on the run. Yet if you want to go deeply into any subject, you need a lot of time, and in particular you need the privilege of wasting time. You need to experiment with unproductive paths, explore dead ends, make space for doubts and boredom, and allow little seeds of insight to slowly grow and blossom. If you cannot afford to waste time, you will never find the truth.

Great power thus acts like a black hole that warps the very space around it. The closer you get to it, the more twisted everything becomes.

If you really want the truth, you need to escape the black hole of power and allow yourself to waste a lot of time wandering here and there on the periphery. Revolutionary knowledge rarely makes it to the center, because the center is built on existing knowledge.

—YUVAL NOAH HARARI,
21 Lessons for the 21st Century

CHAPTER 1

Evan's Notebook

"We are all born superstars."

—LADY GAGA

The start of school in Maine is just a few days away, and while most fifth graders are clinging to the last days of summer, Evan Duprey waits on the granite steps of his house, notebook and pen in hand, ready for a soul-searching book discussion about the importance of looking inward for strength, direction, and power.

His brother Noah is draining jump shots into the portable hoop in the center of the driveway as I arrive. Their mother opens the screen door and waves.

"Hello there, Evan—how's it going?" I say as he climbs into the back of my black Jeep and buckles the seat belt around his tiny waist. He's wearing red athletic shorts and a gray Nike T-shirt. His teeth are white, and his jet-black hair is cut short. He is a boy of summer, ready for a game at any time.

"Thank you," I say to his mom. "We'll be back in a little while." And with that we are off.

Five minutes and three miles later, Evan and I are standing in front of Pear's Ice Cream & Hoagie Shop in Casco Village. The small white building before us was once a service station and auto repair shop. Today, when the single garage door at Pear's rolls upward, two takeout windows appear behind a counter stocked with condiments, menus, and napkins. The ice cream flavors and other food choices are neatly handwritten on the chalkboard wall to the right. Joanne, the owner, jots down our order on a small notepad.

Change is the order of things. It's likely that the first proprietor of this building would not have imagined its purpose today.

Glancing south down the empty road, I can see my boyhood home. Beyond that, I see the house my dad grew up in, the steeple of the church, and the old school I attended as a child. This village is filled with large white houses that were built generations ago, classic Maine homes with real wood siding and brush-applied paint.

We all come from a tribe, and this is where mine lives. The moment and locale of our birth pull on us all. It frames the world and shapes what we see. While our local conditions are real, they are also an illusion. There is actually only one human tribe, and its trajectory transcends time and place. Each soul is here, living a life on Earth, to individuate and, in this way, add a critical piece of perspective to the great human narrative. We are each here to find our own true voice and bring it forth into the world. But the social institutions that surround us are carefully designed to influence our perspectives and channel our voices to enhance an organizational end. Leadership, in many ways, has unfortunately become the art (and increasingly the science) of directing voices.

As a teenager, I was once asked what church denomination my family belonged to. I had no idea what the word *denomination* meant. I thought a church was a church.

"We go to the church in our village," I replied, thinking, *Where else would we go?*

Growing up in the small town of Casco, about halfway between the rocky coast of Southern Maine and the White Mountains of New Hampshire, I had a lot to learn about how connected—yet divided—the tribes of the world had become.

Evan and I are now sitting opposite each other at a green picnic table on the grass near the quiet road. Evan is carefully carving his way through his ice cream to the cone. I have beaten him there, but neither of us is in a hurry. Evan is relaxed and exempt from the constraints of time, just passing another summer day on the slow road to fifth grade.

For me, however, this moment is an accomplishment. It's the middle of the day in the middle of the work week, and I am the CEO of an established forest products company, well known across Maine and nationally in our industry. I could easily be deep into a sequence of "important" meetings and decision-making exercises right now. For me, sitting here is an acquired skill—or rather a *reacquired* skill. I have had to remember what Evan and the school boys of summer already know: how to lose track of time and see a day as something more than just an opportunity to be productive.

As I look at Evan, I am reminded of one of my favorite people, Verola Spider, a grandmother and fourth-generation storyteller from the Pine Ridge Indian Reservation. She lives in the small town of Porcupine, deep within the confines of what the locals call "the Rez," in a remote corner of South Dakota.

* * *

"The Lakota believe that all children are sacred and holy," Verola explains to me one spring day.

We are sitting together at another picnic table under the covered porch at the Singing Horse Trading Post, where I stay when I visit Pine Ridge. It's hot, and Verola is making colorful Lakota medicine wheels from porcupine quills for the annual Sun Dance at Thunder Valley.

It's amazing that she and I are friends. If I had stayed in my lane and stuck to a narrow definition of the word *tribe*, we both would have only had a stereotypic and generalized impression of the world that the other came from. It's disconcertingly easy to judge people we don't know.

"We say that each child is *Wakan Yeja*," Verola says, without looking up from her quill work. "*Wakan Yeja*," she repeats slowly, pronouncing the words for me as I write them down in an old journal. "It means 'sacred one.' Every child is sacred, no matter when or where they enter this world."

Verola pauses, which is customary in conversations at Pine Ridge. When someone stops talking here, it doesn't mean they are done. It often just signals that they are carefully selecting their next words. In the culture I come from, pauses often feel uncomfortable, and many people race to fill them. At Pine Ridge, silence within a conversation is expected and embraced.

"In the old days there was never any child abuse or neglect, because everyone knew children were sacred," Verola says as she selects more colored quills from the clear plastic bag on the table before her. "We have forgotten some of this now, though. Even though we, the Lakota, are the keepers of this knowledge, we can still forget that all children are sacred."

In the old days, I think, repeating Verola's words in my head.

That opening phrase represents an important idea. Wisdom can be lost, and then recovered. Child abuse and neglect are well-known challenges in this community, and the teen suicide rate is among the highest in the nation. Gangs are prevalent and graduation rates are low. Yet this is the same tribe that knows that all children are holy.

Technology is not the only path to progress. Indigenous communities gained awareness of many important truths through their connectivity to nature. These sacred understandings often became foundational values for their society. But even an indigenous community could veer, or be taken, off course.

The Lakota understanding—that each child is sacred—has powerful implications for all modern organizations, including corporations. If each child is sacred, then each adult is also sacred. If each adult is sacred, then work should be organized accordingly. Each person is capable of leading and worthy of being heard.

There is a false premise in business that suggests that the best companies have the best people. This logic implies that the organizations that are not top performers have something less than the best people. This is popular thinking, but untrue. The idea that "the best people win" is a leadership myth that takes pressure off the leaders. The truth is, great people are everywhere. The planet is filled with them. The governance culture the leaders endorse through their actions is the variable that make the difference. An organization's culture either prioritizes the center and collects power or it celebrates the individual human spirit and disperses control.

* * *

"I LIKED YOUR BOOK," Evan says, snapping my awareness back to the picnic table at Pear's.

I smile. Evan is the youngest known reader of my first book, *Not For Sale: Finding Center in the Land of Crazy Horse.* He grabbed his parents' copy one day and dove right in. By summer's end he had finished all 503 pages chronicling my first six trips to the ancestral homelands of the Lakota Sioux tribes.

"That makes me happy," I say. "So, tell me—what is it about the story that interests you?"

"I liked how you went to the reservation to meet the people there, and that no one told you to do this," Evan replies, speaking in a calm, slow cadence reminiscent of the dialogue at Pine Ridge. "You just had this feeling inside of you that going there was something you wanted to do. And even though some people probably didn't understand why, you kept on with it. I liked that. I liked how you listened to your own voice."

Evan reaches into his backpack, pulls out a spiral-bound journal, and opens it to an early page where he has written a list of questions in pencil. He carefully places his notebook on the picnic table, spreading the pages with both hands.

"What are the schools like at Pine Ridge?" Evan asks.

"They are actually very similar to the schools here," I reply.

"Do the kids there speak both English and Lakota?"

"Some do and some don't; it depends on whether Lakota is spoken in their home. There is an effort under way, however, to reintroduce Lakota language to all students at Pine Ridge."

With each answer Evan nods his head and makes a note before proceeding.

"What is the meaning of the Lakota medicine wheel?" Evan asks.

The former history and social studies teacher within me now leaps into action. I reach inside my shirt and pull out the medicine wheel necklace I am wearing.

"So, this is important, Evan," I reply. "There is more to this wheel than first meets the eye. On the surface the wheel is about honoring the sacred powers of the Universe that are out there, beyond our full understanding. The Lakota celebrate Six Great Powers represented by the West, North, East, South, Sky, and Earth. Each has a place on this wheel."

I pause and then point to the center of the wheel, which is appropriately over my heart.

"But here, at the center, a Seventh Power also lives, and it represents the individual human spirit. The Lakota understand that everything we see is related, connected, and sacred. Every person therefore carries a piece of the sacred energy of the Universe within them. But with this knowledge comes responsibility. Awareness of, and respect for, the Seventh Power is essential to a healthy society.

"The Lakota speak of a 'good red road' to walk in life, as well as a black, dark road. The good red road is the one that honors the spirit within ourselves, and within others. This road leads to peace, harmony, prosperity, and growth. The black road is symbolic of the darkness that prevails when we fail to see and respect the Seventh Power's presence within us all. Each individual must look inward to find their true voice and path, while respecting the rights of others to do the same. By focusing on strengthening ourselves from within, we become more present, respectful, and valuable to others."

"That's like sports," Evan says, which reminds me that his father is his basketball coach. "My dad tells us we each have to bring our best individual effort for the team as a whole to be successful."

"Exactly, Evan," I say.

"Why did you always travel to Pine Ridge alone?" Evan asks.

With that I pause, surprised by this deeply personal question.

In one of those rare instances where time seems to dissipate, my mind zips to the past as I reflect upon the years immediately preceding my first trip to Pine Ridge. What did bring me there alone? What was the change I was seeking, and how did it all affect the company I was responsible for leading?

∗ ∗ ∗

ORGANIZATIONS ONLY CHANGE when the people within them—especially the leaders—change. So what drives leaders to change?

Well, in my case, it was necessity.

Something goes wrong and pressure is applied. Eventually the pain of the present becomes the catalyst for a new vision.

Hancock Lumber was established in 1848, and I am part of the sixth generation of my family to work there. Five hundred and fifty other people also work there, sharing responsibility for fifteen locations across Maine and New Hampshire. Our company is integrated across the forest-products value stream. We grow trees, manufacture lumber, build trusses and other construction components, distribute products globally, and retail them locally.

In 1997, my dad, then the leader of our company, died of lymphoma. In 1998, at the age of thirty-two, I became president. At the time, it was difficult to see any other reality. That's what the Hancock boys did. They grew up, and eventually it became their turn to run the company. That's how it had been for two centuries, which was fine by me. I was sure I was ready.

But I wasn't.

In 2007, the national housing and mortgage markets collapsed. In the three years that followed, construction activity in Southern

Maine declined by nearly 66 percent, and our sales fell by almost 50 percent, essentially without losing a customer. It was perhaps the most stressful period in my life, and I felt the responsibility, inherited from previous generations, to protect our tribe. In my younger days, after my dad died, I was determined to become the leader of our company, and now, suddenly, the company itself hung in the balance.

In 2010, at the peak of that collapse, I began to have trouble speaking. In time I learned that I had acquired a rare voice disorder called spasmodic dysphonia (SD). Prior to the onset of my vocal affliction I had been a traditional CEO, ever-present and hard-charging. In many ways, I was the voice of Hancock Lumber. But after SD appeared, that leadership style was no longer possible. I was forced to change.

To get pressure off my broken voice, I began asking lots of questions. The goal was simply to put the conversational responsibility on someone else. "That's a good question. What do you think we should do about it?" became my most common reply.

Eventually, I realized that people didn't need a CEO-centric solution to the vast majority of the problems they identified at work. Although society has been indoctrinated to bring decision-making responsibility to the leaders at the center, people actually know what to do on their own.

As CEO, I discovered that not answering every question was creating better outcomes and broad-based leadership. What began as a strategy to protect my voice soon became a new leadership template for a lumber company in Maine. Every person could be the CEO of their own job.

My learning accelerated in 2012, when I began traveling to the remote and traditionally disenfranchised Pine Ridge Indian Reservation in South Dakota. There I encountered an entire community striving to come back into their own power after centuries of not feeling heard. SD and Pine Ridge joined forces within me to create two important realizations: First, there are lots of ways to lose your voice in this world. Second, leaders have often done more to constrict the voices of others than to liberate them.

According to Gallup's most recent survey, only about 33 percent of American workers feel engaged by their job and company. Some business analysts see this as a threat to corporate productivity, but that's a company-centric view of the data. What I see has deeper social implications. Average Americans who work full-time spend forty-eight hours a week at their job. Work careers last for decades. For that time to be unfulfilling is a wasted opportunity for living, learning, and growing in the moment. Work should be more than just an exercise in economics.

SD and Pine Ridge helped me to realize that engagement at work is low for one simple reason: people don't feel heard. Wouldn't an organization where every voice mattered and everybody led provide more social and economic value than the traditional top-down hierarchy of decision-making by a few?

I began to explore what it would take to encourage this type of power-dispersing transformation within our own company. I started by revisiting the very mission of work itself. I quickly concluded that work should enhance the lives of the people who do it.

So, what's the purpose of life?

From my experiences with SD and Pine Ridge, I reasoned that the purpose of life is to find one's true voice and then bring it forth into the world. Work should advance this universal human quest for self-actualization.

But in a world engineered long ago to serve the organizational center, authentic voices have frequently been restricted, if not silenced outright.

I once gave a talk at a manufacturing company about the importance of making it safe for every voice to feel heard. Afterwards, an employee came up to me and said, "The last time I said what I thought around here, I got sent home for a week."

With that, I had developed a new mission for corporations around the globe, but the first big step was to successfully test, deploy, and refine that purpose within our own company in Maine.

So, at Hancock Lumber, we adopted, in essence, an employee-centric mission. Work should enhance the lives of the people who do it, and a company that facilitates that journey can expect a high degree of employee engagement and customer satisfaction in return.

The culture of an organization is either capital centric or individually focused. In a capital-centric organization the individual is quickly sacrificed for the needs of the larger cause. Another defining characteristic of capital-centric leadership is that there is typically just one accepted truth. In that type of organization, everyone must be cautious about what they say.

When a company makes the betterment of individuals and society the mission, it takes on a cause that can generate broad, organic appeal. The days of ruling from the top for the sole benefit of the empire are running their course. In a world that is flattening rapidly, people want to know their own truth, strengthen their own souls, and speak with their own voices. People will eagerly make big commitments to protect and enhance organizations that prioritize them, but their voice needs to matter. This social transformation will ultimately usher in the decline of the mega-bureaucracy. Organizations that resist the modern human thirst for self-actualization will increasingly find themselves resorting to intimidation, settling for mediocrity, and falling further behind.

To answer Evan's question, Pine Ridge was a place where I could find my own voice. It was a place where I could disconnect from ego, and it forever changed the way I thought about my role as a leader.

* * *

EVAN IS PATIENT. To him, my pause seems warranted.

"I went to Pine Ridge alone to reconnect with the essence of who I was," I say to Evan, finally answering his question. "The partial loss of my voice was both a literal and metaphorical event. I needed to disconnect my internal sense of self from the external roles I played. It was like I was coming home to my inner being, and I needed to do that in a place where nobody really knew me.

"In addition, I just felt really connected to their story. This was a community that had been systematically deprived of its collective voice by self-absorbed leaders from far away. I myself had been dogmatic at times in the past. I had, on many occasions, used my once-strong voice and inherent leadership position to dictate outcomes and exert control over others. I know there were times before SD when people did not feel heard by me. Pine Ridge was in some ways a place where I could begin to make amends. I could call out past injustice. I could begin to reconcile some of my own shortcomings as a leader. I could listen and celebrate the amazing voices that lived there."

Evan nods.

"Your personal experience there reminds me of the Lakota vision quest you wrote about," Evan says.

"I think so too, Evan," I reply. "The vision quest can be as transformational a rite of passage today as it was for past generations. Searching within yourself for direction and purpose will never be outdated. For me, the purpose of the vision quest is to come home to your own personal identity and innate power. You needed to leave your tribe to do this, journeying out into the wilderness alone, often sitting on a hill for days at a time, praying for a vision to come to you. The vision, if received, was a gift from the Great Spirit. In that moment, you were offered a glimpse of your own true path in life. The experience also reinforced the awareness that you are sacred and related to all living creatures. Since you are the only version of you there will ever be, you have a responsibility to live and speak your truth; this is your gift back to the world."

I pause for a moment and take a breath. My SD is catching up with me. When this happens, my words get choppy and occasionally my entire voice just fades out. Sometimes a person can be sitting right next to me and have a hard time hearing anything that I say. Speaking for an extended period can leave me dizzy, sore, and out of breath. But this chat with Evan is meaningful for me, so I'm determined to continue it.

"How did losing some of your voice change your leadership style?" Evan asks.

"A healthy and sustainable society depends upon healthy individuals," I reply. "Losing some of my voice caused me to turn inward and listen to myself more closely. When I did this I began to see lots of ways in which I wanted to grow. SD, it turned out, came to me for a reason. It was a gift that forced change into my life. This caused me to realize that leaders primarily need to work on themselves and make it safe for others to do the same."

"But doesn't that sound selfish?" Evan says. "My teachers, coaches, and parents always say we should think of others before ourselves."

"Of course, we want to help others," I say. "We want our lives to be of value to those around us. The question is how to best do that.

To be valuable to others, we first need to make ourselves as strong as we can possibly be. To make ourselves strong, we look inward."

"How do you go about working on yourself?" Evan asks.

"That's a great question," I say, leaning in as if to tell him a secret. "Because we are all taught to work on others, we're not really given the tools and support we need in order to focus on strengthening ourselves from within. Essentially, it's simple, though. You have to really learn to listen to your own voice—the one that dwells within your heart. But it's easier to become consumed with what other people need to do. It's easier to wait for them to change than to take on the task of changing ourselves."

Evan nods his head.

"Let's go back to your question about how all of this changed my perspective on leadership. I used to think leadership was about directing others. Now I see it differently. Today, I think leadership is primarily about working on oneself. We all want to see the world change in certain ways, but what we fail to realize sometimes is that the path to creating that change lives within us. It's easy to miss this and instead project responsibility onto others. We then become spectators absorbed in what other people are doing wrong. And when this happens, we lose our way—we lose our voice. The big opportunities for growth in our lives come from within. Spasmodic dysphonia and Pine Ridge helped me to see this."

"I understand how losing some of your voice would be a big change," Evan says. "But what was it you saw at Pine Ridge that changed your thinking?"

"At Pine Ridge I saw an extreme example of what can happen when the leaders of one tribe go too far and take too much from another. Our country took more than it needed to from the people who live there. There was room for everyone in the vastness of the American West, but we couldn't see that at the time. Since

American settlers outnumbered the Native tribes, our country just took everything. Why? Because we could."

"It seems like whoever wins a war punishes the other side too much," Evan says.

"That's what the tribe with the most power often does," I reply. "In fact, the Lakota did it themselves. Before the white men began to appear on the northern plains the Lakota had the most people, the most horses, and the most guns. So, they moved farther west, following the great herds of buffalo. The Lakota went on to acquire a vast territory and displace other, smaller tribes, because they were the strongest tribe in the region. But no one likes to remember themselves as the aggressor, so this is not talked about very much at Pine Ridge. This gets right back to the whole point of looking first and hardest at ourselves."

I pause again as Evan writes in his notebook.

"SD and Pine Ridge both came into my life for a reason. Everybody can lead. Everyone is capable of contributing to the success of the tribe. When I started listening more and talking less at Hancock Lumber, I saw that people had great answers and knew what to do. They didn't *need* the CEO to solve the problems they encountered. Society has been indoctrinated in the art of taking decisions 'up the ladder' for approval, but for the most part it's unnecessary. People need lots of encouragement and trust. They don't need lots of supervision.

"I saw the same pattern at Pine Ridge. Virtually everyone I have met there has inspired me. The people who live there are smart, kind, resourceful, proud, caring, and capable. Pine Ridge statistically is the poorest place in America, but it's filled with great people all the same."

"Why do you keep going back to Pine Ridge?" Evan asks. "Are you still searching for something there?"

I smile, lean back, and look out toward the lake across the street.

"You know, that's hard to answer," I reply. "Do you ever feel like there's an important idea, just beyond your reach? Something you're supposed to know, or do, or share, but you can't quite get at it? Well, that's how I feel these days. I think there is something more for me to learn. I mean, I know there's always a lot more to learn, but I'm talking about something very specific—I'm on the trail of an idea that I am supposed to share. I can feel it, but I can't quite see it yet."

My voice trails off. Evan seems satisfied that I am still searching for something. Our conversation is winding down.

"I have a present for you," I say as I reach into my backpack and pull out a colorful Lakota arrow that I bought the last time I was at the Trading Post at Pine Ridge.

Evan takes it from me. "Wow! Thank you," he says. His eyes sparkle as he examines the arrow from tip to feathers. This arrow is more decorative than utilitarian, and Evan's is a hunting family, deeply engaged in the outdoors, so they will appreciate the gesture.

"I have a present for you too," Evan says as he sets the arrow on the picnic table. He takes something from his own small back-pack and hands it to me. "It's a journal," he says, "so you can keep writing. Maybe when you find that important idea you're search-ing for, you can write it down here."

The notebook is white with a single black stripe down the left side near the silver binding. On the cover are words and phrases, each in a different font:

Thoughts

NOTES

Really Great Ideas

MUSINGS

BIG PLANS

On the inside is a personalized note that simply reads: *Here is something to return the favor. Keep on writing! —Evan*

I am touched by this gift. "Thank you so much, Evan! I really love this, and I promise I'll fill it up. The next time I have an important idea that makes me stop and think, I will put it in here. And I'll definitely take it with me to any interesting places I visit."

Evan nods and smiles.

* * *

AFTER I TAKE EVAN HOME, I head back to my office. As I exit his driveway, I whisper out loud, *"Wakan Yeja."*

Suddenly, I feel a sense of urgency to live what I've learned more deeply and consistently. In the five years that have passed since I first began traveling to Pine Ridge, how had I changed? What insights had the experience offered? Had I seized the opportunity and incorporated the small pieces of wisdom that had come my way?

The answer was most certainly yes. And no.

The fresh journal Evan gave me, now resting at my side, was an invitation to keep exploring, growing, and sharing. Our growth only ends when we call off the search. Each of us is woven into the fabric of human existence, and everything in the Universe is related. In traditional Lakota society, everyone had an active role. Each person mattered for their strength, or their experience, or their kindness, or their wisdom. Everyone had something to give, and was expected, even required, to do so. Working on oneself is working on the greater community, on society.

And society is clearly in transition. Globalization connects people as never before. Ideas are communicated at an unprecedented pace. Mobility is expanding. Expectations are rising. Individuals are seeing, saying, and expecting more. But their institutions are slow to respond, entrenched in a top-down, center-first model of leadership. The five big social institutions (family, school, place of worship, place of work, and government) are lagging behind the individual aspirations of their members. Around the globe, memberships in traditional organizations are dwindling, engagement is falling, and participants are rebelling.

The long view of human history could be seen as a slow journey from physical beings to self-identification as spiritual beings. For thousands of years, *Homo sapiens* were fully focused on survival. Food, shelter, and protection from big animals with big teeth dominated each day. But today survival is not a daily concern for most humans (some to be sure, but not most). As safety expands, humans increasingly are turning inward and searching for deeper meaning, purpose, and direction.

For centuries organizations came first and individual aspirations were sacrificed. That model is running its course. It's time for something new.

But how exactly might the new organizational template unfold? In what ways might both leaders and followers be called upon to change?

As I park my Jeep outside Hancock Lumber's modest corporate office, I take a full, conscious breath, grab my notebook, and head inside. I have work to do.

* * *

IN THE WEEKS THAT FOLLOWED, I found myself thinking more and more about the traditional structure and mythology that accompany most modern organizations.

For centuries, leadership has been marketed as something to be done by the few. Across generations, people have been coached and coerced to see themselves as followers. Stories are spun to promote the unique skills and powers of the leaders. The result is that we have been indoctrinated to look externally for solutions to challenges that can ultimately only be answered from within.

The Pine Ridge Indian Reservation is a prime example. Before the reservation era, the Lakota were self-sufficient despite the harsh conditions of the northern plains. In their culture, everyone was called upon to contribute. Leadership was something that all people could provide. But the reservation culture was completely different. The people of Pine Ridge were soon directed to look externally to Washington, DC, where rations were allocated and dispersed. Dependency followed. A once highly adept community became statistically the poorest place in America.

But what really changed?

It was the leadership system.

I have now been to Pine Ridge sixteen times. I can testify with great confidence that the reservation is filled with amazing people. The leadership model matters. Great people are everywhere, but the framework of their organizational system either celebrates or combats the Seventh Power that resides within us all.

Once established, leadership templates are hard to break. Countless self-centered leaders across time have been overthrown only to be replaced by a new self-centered leader. Corruption and ego breed corruption and ego. If you look today at nations that struggle, they are almost always places where the rule of law is selectively applied. In such conditions, corruption prevails and leaders serve themselves.

But what are the origins of these systems?

Almost all of them were previously colonized communities. Colonies were, by definition, places of exploitation. The mother country came first. The local populace was an expendable commodity. The rule of law was selectively applied. When revolution ultimately occurred, the ill-fated traits of self-centered leadership often survived. A broken system changing hands is not progress. That's not the revolution I have in mind.

SD and Pine Ridge combined to help me see that a fresh leadership path is ready to materialize. For centuries, society has been structured to serve the organizational center. But humans evolve. Today, more and more individuals are awakening to the Seventh Power that lives within us all. Organizations that thrive in the future will learn to serve the souls and strengthen the voices of their individual members. This, in turn, will bring forth a revival in organizational excellence as those same individuals reciprocate that care back upon the institutions that celebrate them.

I could feel this transformation in my bones. But I also felt a responsibility to dig deeper and to validate. I had the opportunity to create such a culture within Hancock Lumber. But I also felt a calling to transcend my confines and look broadly, globally, for evidence of this new leadership model unfolding. I wanted to find both new and old examples of communities, organizations, and leaders that were successfully pushing power away from the center.

While a chief dwells within us all, humans still need each other, and working together will continue to hold more potential than operating in isolation. Eliminating organizations is not the answer; re-creating them is. Nevertheless, the pending social transition is a big one. Leadership models in which power is transferred away from the center are potentially threatening to almost everyone, including those who have become accustomed to following. Following has one big advantage: you don't ever have to

take full responsibility—someone else can always be held account-
able if things go wrong, as they often do.

For generations, in different languages and for a variety of
reasons, individuals had been coaxed into ceding a piece of their
own unique voice in exchange for the false safety of following, of
reciting a collective truth. A few set the rules, did the talking, and
collected more power, all in the name of taking care of you. It was
the age of what I call the "single savior leader," and it's a compelling, but false, narrative.

The truth is, great people are everywhere. There is a sacred light
that dwells within us all. Everyone has value to contribute and the
ability to lead. The idea is to turn the corporation inside out. In the
old model, employees were commodities that sacrificed and served
the organization. In the new model, the organization becomes a
conduit for serving individuals. Within a company, for example,
self-actualization, one employee at a time, becomes the goal. Profit,
while enhanced, is now the outcome of a higher purpose.

Two essential learnings are required in order for a new organizational model—driven by the notion of shared leadership—to
unfold. First, we must remove the veil on the traditional organizational premise designed to convince us that power, influence, and
sacredness live "out there," beyond our reach. Until we recognize
this to be a fabricated tale, we cannot transcend it.

This first awareness creates the second understanding: we are
each sacred and powerful where we stand. Human greatness comes
in billions of unique and never-to-be-repeated forms. Companies
must learn to thrive off self-actualization, not thwart it.

Let's make employees the focus of the company. Let's make
human self-actualization the big corporate goal. A lumber company's primary job isn't just the making of lumber; lots of companies
in our industry can do that, and do it well. Our goal is to make

lumber in a manner that advances the self-awareness, self-worth, and self-actualization of the people who do it. That's a big goal that can have broad appeal. Companies that operate with this mission can advance humanity, and thrive in the process.

The understanding that great people are everywhere is the first essential ingredient for the new age of shared leadership. It signals the beginning of a transition from organization-centric to individual-centric thinking.

While this first awareness is, in and of itself, significant, it immediately leads to more questions. If great people are everywhere, why do some organizations thrive while others struggle to survive?

With Evan's notebook in hand, that's the next piece of wisdom I went searching for....

CHAPTER 2

Desert Reckoning

"Culture eats strategy for breakfast."

—PETER DRUCKER

The STAR School sits inconspicuously on the site of a former junkyard at the edge of the Colorado Plateau east of Flagstaff, Arizona. To the west the four sacred peaks of the Navajo Nation cast their shadows. It is a charter elementary and middle school, serving Indian Country, and the most unlikely of places to find a leadership culture that could change not just the world of business, but also the entire planet for the better.

I arrive on a cool morning in early March carrying only the empty notebook Evan gave me. Crushed gravel shifts beneath my feet as I exit my dusty, white rental car. The surrounding cinder hills look otherworldly, which causes me to pause and peacefully take in the landscape. It soon strikes me that this is a place of transitions. It's a place where the mighty ponderosa pine forests give way to the scattered and scented juniper trees. It's a place where the elk cede the ground to the antelope. It's a place where the reservation and non-reservation cultures cross paths. It's a place where a gentle hillside of abandoned cars, rusted refrigerators, and discarded metal parts was transformed into a world-class community of hope. And it's the place where 140 Navajo students each year turn the values of their ancestors into a recipe for modern-day success in a locale where the extraordinary is hard to engineer.

There are just a few vehicles in the parking lot as I make my way toward the small cluster of structures that surround the central playground and outdoor gardens. Windmills turn gently behind the complex, and solar panels face the morning sun in the front. The buildings themselves are single story, adobe colored. Concrete paths guide the primary walking routes, but dirt, soil, bushes, and scattered trees mix freely into the school grounds. The footprint of the facility is soft here by design. Nature and the school itself are intertwined.

Mark Sorensen, the school's cofounder, greets me as I enter the first building on the right. We have met once before and share an affinity for indigenous communities that feel they have not been fully heard. Mark is slender and tall with flowing white hair that darkens slightly at the top of his head where his glasses rest. He is dressed comfortably in blue jeans beneath a black sweater and a casual sport coat.

"While we are a private charter school that sits just outside the boundaries of the Navajo Nation, we do consider ourselves an Indian school," Mark explains as we make our way into his office. "The Navajo community is who we are here to serve. Our mission is for our kids to come out of here feeling empowered and believing in their hearts that they can make a difference."

Values and a strong sense of place come first here, I think, as Mark offers me a seat.

Mark's office is small but filled with the vestiges of curiosity, culture, and inquiry. A red-and-black Navajo rug covers his chair. Another hangs from the wall behind him. A third lies underneath us on the floor. I am sitting in a small black chair opposite his wooden desk. Two other chairs and a bookcase fill the humble room.

We take a moment and just breathe. The pace of dialogue is different in Native communities in the most pleasant of ways. Conversations here are not meant to be timed.

"It's unfortunate that standardized tests don't measure how peaceful it is here and the impact that peacefulness has on our students," Mark says in a soft yet confident voice. With that he begins reflecting on the task of balancing this educational community's unique place and pedagogy with the federal requirements of learning that are pushed down on all schools nationally, regardless of context.

"We teach Navajo language here. We teach Navajo culture here. We teach gardening and living with the Earth, sustainably. We generate our own power, and we grow our own food. In addition, each of our middle school students completes an extensive community service project as a requirement of graduation. These community initiatives require lots of listening to understand what is needed, and then lots of time to implement. And we still have to prepare everyone for the federal testing as a condition of our accreditation. We just make it all happen in a patient and loving way.

"But there is no standardized measurement for the power of peacefulness and self-worth in a child's heart. That's our true purpose. We are not here to prepare for standardized tests. We are here to build human capacity from the inside out."

"If centrally administered standardized tests were the full answer, then every school in America would be a magical place," I reply. "But we both know that's not the secret sauce."

This tiny school is a beacon of light in a place where traditional educational institutions often struggle. Nationally, a minority of students from reservation communities go on to postsecondary education. At the STAR School the number is close to 70 percent. As a result of its performance, this school has a sizable waiting list for entry. Some Navajo families even apply the week their child is born. Something special is brewing at this tiny school and has been for quite some time.

"The community project each graduating student completes is important," Mark says. "Many young people living in Indian Country have a hard time seeing the relevance of education to the world they occupy. We want each of our students to recognize their own worth and understand how their learning can be applied, to the advantage of both themselves and their community."

"Where did the name of the school come from?" I ask.

"STAR stands for 'Service To All Relations,'" Mark explains as he lightly runs his fingers across his white mustache. "At the center of Navajo culture and spirituality is the concept of relationship. We all have many relations, more than most realize. Family, community, clan, nature, animals, spirits, earth, sky—we are related to it all. Learning to see our connectivity is important. When we realize we are connected, we understand we are not alone. It is important to have a sense of place—to belong. Many people around the world have lost their sense of relationship, and that comes at a cost."

Mark pauses. I wait.

"Once our students understand the relationships that surround them, we can begin to talk about service. Being helpful in those relationships is the goal. The idea is simply that you have a responsibility to all of your relations—to all of the people around you, and to nature itself. The Navajo understand that we humans are *of* nature, not above it.

"Today's cultural messages on television are all about how many things you have acquired. But the true meaning of life is not measured by the objects you collect. Life is about understanding your relationships and being of service to the world around you. The goal is sovereignty through service."

Sovereignty is a common term on reservations across the American West. For generations, communities such as these were governed bureaucratically and callously from Washington, DC. The quest to regain sovereignty is the quest to restore the Seventh Power to its rightful place in society. Leadership must be localized in order for a community to function vibrantly. Far too often, leadership has been seen as a zero-sum game. In this narrow context, my power comes at the expense of your power. This perspective is ill suited for the shared leadership potential of the twenty-first century. The truth is, power grows exponentially when it is dispersed. The more power everyone at Hancock Lumber actualizes, the more effective and valuable I, as the CEO, become. Leadership is not finite.

I am writing fast now, keeping pace with Mark. Evan's previously empty notebook is suddenly coming to life. The dialogue is smooth and effortless, as if we both have been destined for this conversation for quite some time.

"Mark, can you take me back and describe what brought you here, and how this school began?" I ask.

"Well," Mark says, leaning back into his chair, "it was the 1970s, and I was pursuing my PhD in multicultural education at the University of Illinois. I was getting ready to do my dissertation, but before I charted a course I wanted to see what Native communities would like to have studied. So I came here to the Navajo Nation to listen, ask questions, and learn."

"Leading through listening," I whisper out loud.

"Yes, it was," Mark says, hearing my own faint words. "In fact, I was so moved by what I heard that I stayed. I gave up my studies and moved here. I began teaching and eventually leading schools on the reservation.

"As the years passed, I started to grow tired of the mediocrity. We were caught in the web of supervision and mandates from the federal, state, and tribal governments. There was just too much bureaucracy, politics, and inertia to get anything magnificent done. Don't get me wrong—we were doing good work, but I could see how it would be so much better if we could eliminate the bureaucratic clutter. So at that point my ex-wife and I did something really crazy. We invested everything we owned, bought this piece of land, and turned it into a school. I think there were eight students here the year we started, and one of them was our son. We threw him right into the experiment as well. That was September 2001, one week before 9/11. Back then I ran the school. Today, I just consider myself the Community Vision Activator."

"What does a Community Vision Activator do, Mark?" I ask, already inspired by the term.

"To have a truly dynamic community school, you first have to know what it is the community wants—I mean, *really* wants," Mark adds. "This can only be accomplished through listening. But somebody then has to take the voice of the community and activate it—give it life. Someone has to articulate the vision, bend the resources toward that vision, and do the work. In our case, what the community wanted was clear. The desire is for their children to feel valued and for that value to become the basic foundation upon which the entire region could someday thrive."

This is a community based on dispersed power. The leaders at this school thrive by strengthening the voices of others. Listening, and accepting students as they are, is the path to reversing generations' worth of top-down control. For decades, the goal of the American government was to "remake" Indian children as whites. American society—and our reservation communities, specifically—is still paying the price for that overreaching.

"Your intentions are so values based," I say. "Where did those values come from, and what are they about?"

"All the core values at the STAR School come from the heritage of this community," Mark says. "The beauty of the Navajo way is extraordinary in how it looks at the world. To the Navajo, everything is interrelated and connected. All creatures are sacred, including humans. Therefore, we all have a place and a purpose. In addition, we all have a responsibility to that which we are related. All we needed to do here was extract the knowledge that has existed for a long, long time and reactivate it."

The door to my left opens, and a man enters.

"Kevin, please meet Thomas Walker Jr.," Mark says, as he stands to greet his friend.

I stand as well. Thomas and I shake hands, and then he sits in the chair against the wall, to my left. Thomas is of medium height with short dark hair, brown skin, and a slight mustache. He wears blue jeans, a black shirt, a black coat, and glasses.

"Thomas has been one of the leaders of our school and community for many, many years," Mark says. "He was involved from the very beginning and has given us wisdom and guidance every step of the way. Today he is a member of our board and a Navajo Nation peacemaker. I thought it would be helpful if Thomas told you a little bit about the peacemaking tradition of the Navajo. That tradition is central to the culture of our school."

"My dad used to tell me that out there on the horizon, where the sky meets the earth—that is where we human beings live,"

Thomas says. "We are at the center. We live at the intersection of the sky and Mother Earth. It's a powerful place to be."

That's the Seventh Power of the Lakota. All indigenous communities, through their immersion in nature, seem to acquire similar knowledge.

"To understand either our school community or the philosophy of Navajo peacemaking, you must understand the concept of ké," Thomas continues. "Ké is the understanding and honoring of our relationships. In Navajo culture, this is done first through clan. For example, my clan is the Salt People. If someone is a member of my clan, I see my relation to them and I honor that relation in all forms. I honor my brother by honoring his children. That's our way."

Thomas takes a moment to remove and clean his glasses before continuing.

"While clan is powerful, ké is about more than clan. Ké is about understanding our connectivity to all things. We are connected to Mother Earth. We are connected to Father Sky. So we have relationships to all that exists in the world around us. As a result, we are never alone. We are never disconnected."

"This is why I tell our students to be good in all settings, even when you may think you are alone," Mark says, and then laughs. "The spirits are always watching."

"Prayer is about the belief that these entities that surround us can assist us," Thomas says. "Our understanding of ké drives our values, which then show up in our ceremonies. There can't be ceremony without values."

"Everywhere you turn here, you have relations," Mark says. "This is what pulled me into the Navajo community. Ké pulled me in. When I came to understand ké, I came to understand that I had responsibilities. Ké teaches us to be there for one another through everything."

"Sometimes there are still disagreements," Thomas says. "Let's say two members within a clan have a disagreement in which people are saying or doing hurtful things. Pretty soon distance between people is created. Now we have a problem. This is where peacemakers come in. The peacemaker's role in Navajo society is to pull the relationship back together and eliminate the distance."

"Is there a process to peacemaking that others could follow?" I ask. "The planet could certainly use some fresh perspective on transcending disputes and restoring our sense of relationship."

"The process has seven steps," Thomas replies. "Together, the steps are designed to restore relations rather than assign guilt or punishment. First, the peacemaker requests spiritual assistance. This is done through an offering prayer that asks for the best possible outcome. Next, everyone present acknowledges how they are connected and related. Our relationships are identified before our problems are described. This is intentional because it reminds us that the relationship is more important than the problem."

This makes so much sense, I think.

"Then the peacemaker reviews the ground rules for everyone to honor and follow. For example, there can only be one speaker at a time, and no one may put anyone else down. Everyone is asked to talk about only their own feelings and refrain from judging the other person. Then each participant describes the specific problem as they experienced it. Everyone is free to speak for as long as they like. No one is interrupted. As this happens, the peacemaker listens and guides the conversation toward the areas of common ground, like the desire for all parties to feel respected. After all the voices are heard, the peacemaker facilitates the creation of a specific set of steps to be taken to restore the relationship. These steps are agreed upon, and everyone then makes an apology. Finally, a statement of gratitude is given for the relationship that has been restored."

Thomas goes quiet. Mark is leaning back in his chair, nodding his head. I am inspired.

"The simplicity of that system is elegant," I say. "First, there is the understanding of relationship. Second, there is the responsibility to that which we are related. This provides such a clear road map. A dispute, by definition, is a disturbance in relationship. Dispute creates distance. Peacemaking deconstructs the distance, thereby restoring the relationship. It's lovely."

The door behind me opens once again as Mark stands.

"Kevin, meet Pauline Butler."

I stand and shake hands with Pauline.

"Pauline is a former parent here," Mark says. "She is also a member of our board, and the Coordinator of Community Happiness here at school."

"Another great role," I reply, "like Community Vision Activator. What does being the Coordinator of Community Happiness entail, Pauline? How did you get that job?"

"It's simple, really," Pauline explains, sitting down between Thomas and me in the room's last available chair. "My job is to make sure people are comfortable and happy in all settings. In the classroom, on the bus, in the garden, at lunch—people need to feel comfortable and happy in order to learn and grow to their full potential. I love my job. I know every child in our school."

Pauline pauses and laughs with satisfaction. She is wearing black jeans and a gray sweatshirt. A Wonder Woman cartoon key chain hangs around her neck.

"In terms of how I got the job—I just really believed in this school and got involved. From there it grew. The kids don't really know what I do. They just see me everywhere."

"One of the most powerful components of the peacemaking process is the simple act of listening and feeling heard," Mark says.

"When people learn to sit without judgment and listen to the feelings of the other side, it changes things. 'Well, I didn't know this situation affected you in that way' is a common response. 'I'm sorry.' There's a natural reconciliation that happens once people sit still and listen to how the situation makes others feel."

"What are the core values of the peacemaking process itself?" I ask.

Mark looks at Thomas, deferring to him.

"Our process is guided by four Rs," Thomas says. "Respect, relationship, responsibility, and reasoning—these are the four Navajo values of peacemaking. These are also the four core values of our school."

"Can you tell me a bit about each?" I ask.

"Respect is demonstrated by listening," Thomas says. "Listening allows us to recognize that each person has something important to offer."

"At its highest level, respect might be thought of as the ability to see and acknowledge the light and beauty in each person's face, including your own," Mark adds.

Thomas nods his head. The Lakota and Navajo views in this regard are quite similar. *Indigenous wisdom is indigenous wisdom,* I think.

"The second R is relationship," Thomas continues. "This is simply the recognition that the other person over there is not separate from me, but that we are interconnected. Then there is responsibility. This is looking for ways in which *you* can make a situation better, and acting on that responsibility without being led or told to do so. Finally, there is reasoning, which is the awareness to think things through before you act. It's the ability to realize our own capabilities as problem solvers. Together the four Rs create the capacity for individuals to take care of themselves and add value to the lives of others."

"It's no wonder this school has become so successful," I say. "The mission is so broad-based and focused on the individual student as a human being in the context of their larger world."

"K'é is a map for how to live," Thomas says. "The one big idea is that we can solve our own problems."

"When we start looking at children as powerful beings, then who are we not to expect great things?" Mark says.

"If we can build a beautiful school where there used to be a junkyard, anything is possible," Pauline adds.

The conversation is now traveling in a rhythmic circle.

"Once a person starts down the path of self-empowerment, you begin to see more and more potential and possibility," Thomas says. "The power doesn't come from somebody else telling us what to do. It's just about realizing we are each powerful beings as we are."

"Being intentional about the culture within an organization is critical," Mark says. "We decided early on to create space in each school day to work on the culture. This is a challenge in a world of standardization where everyone wants to measure you by your test scores, but despite that, we hold the space open. You must hold the space for the values to mature and be practiced. And we can't expect the kids to practice these values if we don't model them ourselves as teachers."

Suddenly it hits me: getting the culture right is essential to the new paradigm of shared leadership. The federal government puts a premium on standardized test scores as a benchmark for educational excellence, but the STAR School has a higher calling. Surely reading, writing, and math proficiency matter, but that's not the reason why this school exists. This school is driven by a more ambitious mission that leverages the traditional wisdom of the Navajo Nation and makes it relevant for the modern age. The mission of this school is to help each child find their worth and see their connectivity.

"Everyone has sacred value," I say. "This is a fundamental truth that some organizations have lost sight of. When I travel around Hancock Lumber, I don't see employees—I see people."

This remote school exists to honor and strengthen the sense of worth in each individual student. When this happens the school becomes successful by default, but the success of the institution is not the goal.

"It's up to us," Thomas says. "If we don't succeed, we have no one else to blame."

The wisdom and truth of the Seventh Power is flowing freely right now.

"But we chose that," Thomas continues. "We created this school because we chose to step in and replace the state ourselves. That's the real meaning of self-determination. The power we seek lives within. It's not out there, in a tribal, state, or national capital somewhere."

* * *

An hour later I am standing on the corner in Winslow, Arizona, just as the Eagles' first hit song describes. As I reflect on that iconic song, "Take It Easy," I contemplate Mark Sorensen's legacy as someone who certainly found a place to make his stand.

After relishing my brief stop in this lonesome desert town, I head south on Route 87 toward Payson and soon find myself in a seemingly endless forest of ponderosa pines.

There are no cars in front of me and none behind. I have this road to myself, and as I placidly drive along, I contemplate my

visit to the STAR School. So many leadership lessons, initially discovered through SD and Pine Ridge, were played back to me this
morning by Mark, Thomas, and Pauline.

I scan beneath the pines and across the scattered snow patches
for elk. Even though the temperature is forty-one degrees, my
window is down. I want to be as close to nature as possible, and
the cool wind careening across my left arm is one way to feel the
connectivity I seek. The road before me bends and descends. Time
momentarily loses meaning, and I contemplate both the implications and integration of what I have learned.

Organizations are ultimately defined by their culture, and
leaders have the most power to create it, consciously or otherwise.
Leaders matter because culture matters.

I have a picture at home from 1991, my first year working at
Hancock Lumber. I'm wearing blue jeans and a red sweatshirt
with the phrase *Our people make the difference* printed in white,
underneath our company logo. As much as I love what this quote
represents, I have come to believe that it's not quite true. I think
the *culture* is what actually makes the difference, because great
people are everywhere. There is no single department, corporation, state, nation, race, or tribe that has cornered the market on
great people. The truth is, great people are abundant and equally
dispersed around the world. Even a cursory look at history rein-
forces the controlling impact culture has had on the behavior and
performance of tribes.

Germany in the twentieth century is but one of many stark
examples. First, there is Germany under the Nazi culture, defined
by unimaginable yet calculated atrocities. Then, after World War
II, there is an extended period of a Germany divided between east
and west. West Germany, democratic and free, would become
one of the strongest economic engines in the world, while East

Germany would fall into the autocratic, centrally planned, government-first orbit of the USSR. West Germany would prosper, and East Germany would stumble along until it collapsed under its own weight.

I traveled to Berlin in the late 1980s, before the wall came down. It was sobering in the extreme to see the barbed wire and gun towers that kept East Germans from fleeing to West Berlin. But what was the real difference between the two Germanys after World War II? It couldn't be that the "best" Germans all ended up in the west. The difference was culture. Germany after World War II was filled with amazing human beings on both sides of that arbitrary line. One Germany celebrated and protected the power of the individual human spirit, while the other sacrificed and exploited it.

Germany is but one of many historic examples that demonstrate the impact culture has on a divided tribe. In 1953 one country became two when Korea was separated along the 38th parallel. North Korea would follow the path of another self-centered "all glory to the state" dictatorship. South Korea would go on to become free and democratic. North Korea would fence itself in, and imprison, torture, or shoot citizens who threatened, or were perceived to threaten, the regime. Today, the differences between the two Koreas are so startling that it's hard to imagine it was all one country just a few generations ago. While the population of South Korea today is approximately double that of North Korea, its economic output is more than thirty-five times larger than that of its counterpart. Life expectancies in South Korea today are, on average, more than ten years longer than in North Korea. Yet in 1952, it was all the same tribe. In the year the country was divided, the "good" Koreans did not all end up in the south while the "less good" Koreans remained in the north. Great Koreans were, and

are, equally dispersed. The entire difference between the two countries is the culture imposed by leadership.

The Pine Ridge Indian Reservation is another example of the
difference culture makes. Before America's Western expansion,
the Sioux tribes living west of the Missouri River were healthy,
strong, and self-sufficient. But after generations of conquest, colonization, and genocide, today's Sioux reservations are among the
poorest places in America. This is not a coincidence, but rather
a consequence of the leadership structure and values that were
imposed by the American conquerors. The people of Pine Ridge
have the same innate human gifts and capabilities today as they
did before the reservation era. What changed? The culture of the
community changed. Who changed it? Those who had the most
power—the leaders.

To read the stories of how the reservations of the American
West were established and then mismanaged by the federal government is hard sledding. Extreme racism, corruption, inefficiency,
and a general lack of care would be the hallmarks of the system for
a hundred years. The reservations were managed from Washington, DC, promises were routinely broken, resources were always
scarce, and the residents were trained to sit and wait for rations to
arrive and be administered. For more than a century the tribes of
the region lived under a gawky, bureaucratic, and grossly ineffec-
tive system of government that created extreme dysfunction and
hardship. Broken patterns of governance are often inherited, and
when control of the reservations was transitioned more fully to
the tribes in the 1960s and 1970s, the corruption, inefficiency, and
ineffectiveness of government survived.

Culture matters. Leaders drive culture. Therefore, leadership
matters.

Great people live everywhere; the planet is actually filled with them. It is self-serving for leaders to say, "If only we had better people, we could achieve more dynamic results."

I saw a magnificent example of this today. Despite their financial and geographic limitations, the STAR School achieves excellence in a place where both the painful pull of the past and the inertia of government are strong. Yet the school thrives.

Why?

It's the culture the leaders have created. This morning I saw three leaders filled with the bliss that comes from following your own voice. Mark, Thomas, and Pauline are rewriting the playbook on how to create a great reservation school. Had they stayed within the bureaucratic boundaries and played by the established rules, the school might have scratched and clawed its way to average results. The STAR School is an exceptional example of the Seventh Power at work. Releasing your own true voice is the only way to create something new.

It's so important to get the purpose of an organization right. The STAR School teaches spelling and math, but that's not the mission. The mission is to create a sense of self-worth, connectivity, and empowerment in the hearts of their students. Mark spoke this morning about the importance of constantly making time for culture and values at a school measured federally only by its test scores. Contemplating a marvelous mission that transcends both ego and entrenched statistics is critical to organizational vibrancy.

When I was young, I subconsciously saw our company as a way to prove my worth. In those early years I was in a power-collecting mode. I was everywhere within the organization. Presiding over decisions and making lots of presentations and pronouncements. The problems with this model were acute, but I could not see them. When the boss owns all the important decisions, responsibility for the outcomes is not shared. When my perspectives were questioned, I got dogmatic. As a result, the organization became quiet. Discussions were not vibrant; decision-making was not broad-based, and responsibility for outcomes was limited.

But then I lost some of my voice, and change was thrust upon me.

For me, the primary mission of our company today is to be valuable to the people who work there. A company's true worth is not defined by revenue growth or profitability. While these are important metrics for our business, they are but outcomes of a higher purpose. If we can make Hancock Lumber a great place for the employees, it will become a great place for the customers, and everything else we care about will follow.

Hancock Lumber is not about making lumber any more than the STAR School is about test scores. Lumber is important. Test scores are important. But the mission that defines why we exist is much bigger, and that is our differentiator.

Modern organizations are finding it challenging to engage their members. People are restless because there is a growing understanding that something better is possible.

Advancing the human condition should be the mission of all organizations. An entity is only valuable if it is committed to improving the lives of its stakeholders by making them more powerful than the organization itself. Organizations that serve the center are, well, self-centered.

* * *

IT'S NOW EARLY EVENING, and I am out for a sunset walk on Shadow Mountain Road just north of Phoenix, not far from my hotel. Tomorrow I am going home and taking the wisdom of the Navajo peacemakers with me.

I feel light as I walk along, almost as if I am floating. I have been given a gift today by the STAR School. Beautiful homes are scattered about, but all I can see is the desert itself and the sky above. To my left the sun is descending toward Squaw Peak. To my right the shadows are making their ritualistic evening climb up Mummy Mountain. Behind me Camelback Mountain holds its rugged form. Dirt, rocks, flowers, cactus, and pines share the landscape. Birds sing as they dart about. Day yields to night. The air is dry, and a gentle breeze blows. I feel completely absorbed.

The narrow, paved road weaves left, then right. There are no cars in sight. It's just me and the desert.

Suddenly, I stop in my tracks as an idea manifests. Instantly, as if greeting an old friend, I know it to be the foundational clue I have been searching for, as well as the genesis of the STAR School's success. The idea is profound in its simplicity. The fundamental truth, that triggers all other truths, is finally before me.

"Oh, my goodness," I whisper.

In nature, power is dispersed.

For a moment time is lost as I stand alone with this elegant insight that connects me to all the world.

As I regain broader awareness, the evening shadows are scampering up the cactus-covered ridgeline to my right with the confidence that millions of years of repetition affords. Darkness is coming to take this desert once again, and there is no possibility that this ritual can be avoided.

In nature, power is dispersed.

At some point I find myself walking again. I'm not sure when this happens, because my mind is racing with the implications of this short sentence.

Suddenly I get nervous. What if I forget this five-word sequence before I get back to the hotel and can write it down? As crazy as that might seem to you, the threat feels real, and I begin to sweat. My short-term memory is unreliable, and I know it. A journal is my only defense against this vulnerability.

But my journal can't save me now, and that gives me anxiety. The notebook Evan gave me is over a mile away on a coffee table in front of a television. The fear of a mental lapse intensifies, so I keep whispering the sentence to myself as I accelerate my pace and cut through the desert's last light.

> *In nature, power is dispersed.*
> *In nature, power is dispersed.*
> *In nature, power is dispersed.*

I repeat those five words, occasionally contemplating their implications, but mostly just trying to remember them. I feel like I'm carrying a torch into a windswept canyon. My ability to see is one gust away from going out. So just to be safe, I shorten the sentence to a phrase, feeling that it improves my chances of retention:

> *Power is dispersed.*

The birds are rejoicing, and the trees are celebrating with the wind as I walk. The sun has now been fully absorbed by the rugged, rocky ridge to my left. The scene is surreal, and I am the only human in sight. I feel grateful. It all reminds me of something Albert Einstein once said: "Look deep into nature, and then you will understand everything better."

But stay focused, I think. Don't worry about Einstein right now; you can always google what he said later.

The Universe has patterns; one might even call them rules. When we align with these rules the Universe conspires to help us.

When we resist or ignore the flow of nature, we make life more difficult than it needs to be. Everyone who has ever paddled a mighty river knows that when you fight the current, you exert a lot of energy but don't get very far.

We all can learn to glimpse the sacred energy of the Universe, and I just had a peek right here, on Shadow Mountain Road. Seeking is the biggest step in finding.

In nature, power is dispersed.

* * *

THE EVENING WALK HAS ENDED, and I'm sitting on a patio chair looking up at the silhouette of Camelback Mountain against a clear night sky. A full moon is rising to my left, and the stars, one by one, are making their presence known.

Of course, power is dispersed in nature. Everything I saw during my walk this evening was important to every other thing I saw. The soil is critical to the plants and the trees. The plants and trees are essential to the birds and the insects. The existence of small animals is intertwined with larger ones. Although some creatures become active during the night, they are nonetheless in partnership with those who exert more energy during the day. The moon follows the sun. The mostly dry days and the occasional bouts of rain are perfectly balanced to support that which lives here. Nature, it turns out, does not have a headquarters or central office. The wonders of nature are everywhere, equally dispersed.

"K'é", I whisper. "Navajo wisdom."

No single tree is the CEO of all the other trees. No single bird sets the agenda for all the other birds. There is no central office in the desert. How could a truth this simple be so elusive? How could a pattern this obvious have kept me searching for so long? It all makes me laugh. I feel relieved. As I reflect and muse, the lights of Paradise Valley and suburban Scottsdale twinkle in the warm night air. My mind wanders now exponentially, filling with examples of how balance—the harmony nature seeks—is achieved through power dispersal. Creatures big and small, adversarial and collaborative, dance in my head.

Power is dispersed between the lion and the gazelle. If the lions could eat all the gazelles, they would. But they can't. The lions can only catch some of the gazelles. If all the gazelles could outrun the lions, they surely would. But they can't. What's more, the lion and the gazelle actually need each other. Both species would lose their own balanced place in the savannah if the other were not present. Likewise, power is also dispersed between the grizzly bear and the salmon. Grizzlies can catch some of the salmon, some of the time, as they fight their way upstream to spawn, but they can't catch all the salmon. In return, all the salmon can't avoid all of the bears. Power is also dispersed between the forests and the grasslands. If the trees could grow everywhere, they would, but they can't. If the grass could overtake every forest, it would, but it can't.

On and on I go as I sit under what is now a bright desert sky full of stars. Everywhere, in endless quantities, the examples are suddenly clear.

In nature, power is dispersed.

The tie-in back to the future of organizational development is also clear. Humanity is determined to move with the rhythm and rules of nature. This knowledge lives in k'é and is being brought back into the light for the modern age at places like the STAR School.

The whisper of nature is stirring the planet. Each person is sacred and capable of leadership. Fewer and fewer people are willing to support organizations that deny this fundamental truth.

In nature, power is dispersed.

All this could easily be misconstrued. Power dispersal does not mean equality. Nature has never been, nor will it ever be, a guarantor of equality. In fact, nature only guarantees the opposite.

No two creatures are the same. Not every species can survive every climatic event. If you are a slow gazelle, you will probably not live as long as a fast gazelle. Power is dispersed, but nature never guarantees individual outcomes. That's what keeps each creature alert and the entire system evolving, progressing, and improving. Planet Earth is a place of tremendous change and growth precisely because each participant must be alive, alert, and engaged in order to survive. If nature had designed itself to guarantee outcomes, it would have crushed its own evolutionary mission. We each must own the hard work required to bring out the best of who we are, regardless of circumstance.

On an organizational level, leaders have a choice: they can either be agents for releasing and strengthening the voices of others, or they can devote themselves to blunting the human spirit.

The culture at the STAR School is designed to disperse power and celebrate the individual student. It's a winning formula because it's aligned with nature's most sacred rule. This school is using its community's own indigenous wisdom to create a superior performance. How was this done? Through the creation of a culture that first serves the student as a human being—not the Department of Education.

* * *

I HAVE A DEAR FRIEND NAMED DEBORAH DOOLEY. A clinical psychologist with a PhD, she's a transcendent thinker from the San Francisco Bay area. When it comes to looking inward and searching one's soul for direction, she is a trusted mentor.

I was introduced to Deborah nearly a decade ago by my mother, who hired her to do an evolutionary astrology reading for me. The reading of my natal chart was a profound experience. Deborah, I would soon learn, is all about helping her clients acquire the skills necessary for heightening their self-awareness.

The idea of looking at myself in a consistently objective way was new territory for me. I had been focused, like most people, on the external. My attention was often on others and what they were or weren't doing. I had yet to learn how to examine my own patterns of behavior. But as I spent time speaking with Deborah, I caught on pretty quickly. I don't mean to say that I was a master student; I wasn't. It's just that the idea of self-reflection as a path for growth struck a deep chord.

As soon as I returned home from the desert, I was excited to contact Deborah and share what I had learned about how the dispersal of power is wired into the rhythm of the Universe itself and the implications this held for progressive leadership thinking.

The following week I'm sitting in my office at Hancock Lumber, on the edge of Pleasant Lake in Casco. Spring has yet to arrive in Western Maine, and the scene outside is cold and gray. It's 4:00 p.m. (EST), and our Skype appointment has just begun.

Deborah's long white hair flows unrestrained as she greets me with a warm smile. She always gives me the opportunity to go first, so I dive right in and tell her about my learnings at the STAR School and the message that came my way on Shadow Mountain Road.

"You're missing one essential point," Deborah says after listening like a peacemaker to all I have to say. "The lions and the grizzly bears aren't driven by ego. They eat simply to fill a basic need. When they are full, they stop eating."

There is a long pause as Deborah lets this idea sink in.

"Humans are easily driven by ego. Consider what you wrote in your first book, Kevin—the story of America's Western expansion. We didn't just kill some of the buffalo; we killed *all* the buffalo. Think about that. We killed *all the buffalo*. Why did we do that?"

Deborah is looking right at me with those penetrating eyes that do not allow truth to hide. When she looks at me like this, I feel like she can read my mind. Sometimes it makes me look away before I take a deep breath, gain some courage, and reengage.

"Greed and ego drove this," Deborah says. "It wasn't necessary for our survival. We did not need to kill *all* the buffalo to survive. That was just greed and ego, unchecked."

"If greed and ego drive overreaching, then self-awareness must drive restraint," I say to Deborah after a pause.

"Yes," Deborah replies.

"So the challenge is to become more self-aware," I say. "We must each work to make ourselves more self-aware before we can be of real help to others."

"Yes," Deborah says.

That wisdom lives in the four Rs of the STAR School: respect, relationship, responsibility, and reasoning.

"Knowledge from the past can be the gateway to the future," I say.

"Yes," Deborah says one final time.

* * *

THE STAR SCHOOL IS GIVING FRESH LIFE to some ancient Navajo wisdom, and it represents a path toward the future that any community on Earth could follow.

"Once a person starts down the never-ending road of self-empowerment, you begin to see more and more potential and possibilities," said Thomas. "If we don't succeed, we have no one else to blame."

Thomas, the Navajo peacemaker, understands k'é. He knows that nature disperses power and that each person carries a piece of the sacred light of humanity within them.

"The idea is that we can solve our own problems," Thomas declared.

Pauline also knows this. That's why she is the Coordinator of Community Happiness who knows every child by name.

Mark Sorensen knows this as well. As Mark said to me from the comfort of his blanketed chair, "When we start looking at children as powerful beings, then who are we not to expect great things?"

Mark knows what Verola Spider knows. Every person is *Wakan Yeja*. It's not just the select few at the bureaucratic center that hold special skills and powers. We are all sacred and holy. Leaders and organizations that defy this unalterable truth are on borrowed time as they can only rule from a position of intimidation and fear.

Everyone has value. Everyone is sacred. An organization either embraces or resists this truth. If an organization celebrates the human spirit, it will disperse power, not collect it. In the old leadership model the members of the tribe were asked to put themselves second, behind the aspirations of the organizations they served. In the new age of shared leadership, the empire melts away in service to others. This, ironically, is the new path to institutional loyalty. When I, as an individual, recognize that the institution cares about me, I will reciprocate my care back upon the institution. I will sacrifice—not because I have to, but because I choose to. Organizational discipline increases when the individual is honored and each voice is set free.

The culture of modern organizations must be inverted to first serve, strengthen, and honor the individual. This, in turn, vitalizes the organization. It's the culture that makes the difference.

This awareness is the second lesson of the age of shared leadership.

CHAPTER 3

The Whispers Within

> *"I think all creativity comes out of an encounter
> with silence."*
>
> —MATTHEW FOX

The last time I was on a platform like this one, I was trying to hide. I was singing in my elementary school Christmas concert, quite certain I had the worst voice in my class. My parents and many other families from across our community were there, listening to their children perform iconic Christmas songs on the last day before holiday break.

This is a coincidental moment for me to reflect on my brief and unmemorable chorus career, because today I'm in the self-proclaimed "city of music." On this sunny spring Saturday, Nashville is hosting the annual symposium of the National Spasmodic Dysphonia Association (NSDA), and I am its keynote speaker. There are lots of ways to lose your voice in this world, and that understanding is what brings me here.

During the morning session some of the most respected physicians, therapists, and research scientists in the field of vocal disorders shared their expertise. Industry leaders from the nearby Vanderbilt Voice Center, the UCLA School of Medicine, and the University of Minnesota all discussed what they've learned across decades of clinical work with SD patients. Now it's my turn to talk, and the group is about to hear from one of its own.

"Hello. My name is Kevin Hancock, and I have spasmodic dysphonia."

SD is rare, affecting perhaps twenty-five thousand people in North America, so most days those of us with the disorder never hear another person that sounds quite like we do. But today is different. Today this room is filled with people who share the bond of a broken voice.

Spasmodic dysphonia manifests itself through speech, but its origins are neurological. When I talk, certain neurons in my brain misfire. When this happens the muscles around my Adam's apple spasm and contract involuntarily. At that point, forcing out even a few short sentences becomes a physical chore. I strain and sometimes even get light-headed. At its worst, SD feels as if a seat belt has been fastened to the center of my neck and tightened with every word.

To the listener, SD can sound a bit like a bad cell phone connection, where the signal keeps cutting in and out. Certain sounds or entire words go missing, and my voice becomes guttural and choppy, or extremely faint and reduced to a whisper. It's a disorder that makes speaking a challenge, and most people with SD respond by doing less of it.

There are two primary treatments for spasmodic dysphonia: one is chemical, and the other is spiritual. Four to five times a year I travel to Massachusetts Eye and Ear in Boston where my friend Dr. Song gives me a Botox injection aimed toward a precise but hard-to-locate spot in my larynx. Botox is a muscle relaxant that coaxes my vocal system into not overfiring. When the Botox is effective, its benefits can last for a couple of months at a time, and during these periods my voice can function fairly normally. But Botox for SD is an inexact science that sometimes brings relief and sometimes misses the mark. In any case, Botox is not a cure, but rather a temporary inhibitor of the symptoms of SD.

On the spiritual side, if you have SD you learn that the more you can relax the inner/center core of your being, the better your voice performs. Tightness of body or mind exacerbates SD. Fluidity of breathing and mindfulness reduces the symptoms. In this way someone with SD has a built-in self-awareness barometer. SD calls you inward—but as it is with all callings, you must take action and respond.

SD is so rare that it was two years after onset before I even met another person who had it. But today I am happily surrounded by people with SD. All of us, as conference participants, are taking energy and courage from each other's presence. It's always uplifting to realize that you are not alone.

The stage I stand on is approximately three feet high and seems too tall for the room, which leaves me feeling conspicuously close to the ceiling, like Alice in Wonderland. In addition, I have to be precise with each step as the entire contraption squeaks and rattles at the slightest disturbance. This stage, you might say, has its own healthy voice. So I practice what my friend and event producer, Adam Burke, once taught me to do in any public speaking venue: I pick a spot near the front of the stage, disperse my weight, plant my feet, and stand my ground.

"I am truly happy to be here," I say, with all the noticeable symptoms of SD on display. "Everyone in this room has an important story to share, and your presence here says a great deal about your resolve."

The ballroom we occupy is large, windowless, and nondescript. Well over two hundred people fill the majority of available seats, and the collective commitment in the room is palpable. This bighearted and determined group descended on this city with purpose.

After surveying the room, I hold out a copy of E. B. White's timeless children's story, *The Trumpet of the Swan*.

The world is full of talkers, but it is rare to find anyone who listens. And I assure you that you can pick up more information when you are listening than when you are talking.

"You can say that SD limits speaking, or you can say that it increases listening," I say, setting down the story of the young trumpeter swan without a voice.

"SD increases the amount of time we spend listening to others, but it also increases the amount of time we spend listening to ourselves. And while it definitely creates certain challenges, it also unveils opportunities. There can be a purpose in all of this if we choose to track it down.

"For example," I say, "I believe my voice disorder came to me with intention. It was a gift from my own soul." ·

I pause for a moment so that the idea of SD as a blessing can be considered. As I scan the room, I can tell that people are taking in this possibility and contemplating their own experience.

"SD helped me stop, sit still, and listen. When this happened I began to hear whispers," I say. "I find it ironic that my external speaking voice had to dissipate in order for my internal voice to become stronger. For the first time in my adult life, I realized that my sense of self-identity needed to separate from the public roles I played. In Maine and across our industry I was a well-known CEO of a well-regarded company. But when I truly began to venture inward, there was no CEO there. There was just a human being and a voice transcendent of the physical world of doing, creating, and accomplishing. It was at that moment that I realized for the first time that being a CEO was just a role I played. Seeing myself from the inside out was the gift that SD gave me.

"In time, SD also changed the way I think about leadership. Leaders could actually increase their effectiveness by working harder on themselves, losing some ego, sharing the stage, and listening more. These realizations ran counter to most everything I had been taught about how leaders should operate. My dad had been an iconic leader in his time. If you thought of Dave Hancock, you thought of Hancock Lumber, and vice versa. The person and the company were inseparable. I grew up with that traditional model of the highly visible, ever-present leader. And I was on that same course…until my voice gave out.

"What I initially perceived as an illness and a liability was actually a gift. The limitations of my own voice were actually a leadership invitation to strengthen the voices of others. The idea of creating a company where everyone leads suddenly became the new mission and an exciting opportunity.

"Indigenous communities have long known that nature disperses power," I say. "The sacred energy of the Universe lives in all creatures, great and small. Truth resides in the gathering of all voices. People around the world are losing interest in having their truth handed down to them by a leader from above. Most importantly, SD helped me realize that leadership is first and foremost about what I need to do. When we strengthen ourselves, we change the world.

"I might have missed all of this without SD," I continue. "Despite the fact that SD can be a pain in the neck, it has been a blessing. SD has given me much more than it has taken away."

I pause, intentionally slowing the pace. The room is united in thought, and I can see some tears.

"I have a question to pose," I say, in my softest possible voice. "What if SD chose you for a reason? If SD came to you with a purpose, what might that purpose be?"

This room full of broken voices is now silent.

"Could it be that SD actually came your way to free your voice, not restrict it?" I continue. "It is ironic, but SD can actually be a voice-liberating condition. Consider the invitation that SD has extended to you. I'm sure it's there, and I'm sure it's personal. It's a message just for you that only you can hear. But we must search for the message, find the trail, and do the work. As my friends at Pine Ridge often say, 'The spirits will only meet you halfway.'"

As I exit the fragile stage, I feel content. I am grateful for this opportunity to be heard.

* * *

MY VIEW OF LEADERSHIP WAS FOREVER ALTERED by my voice condition. I had to talk less, which created the opportunity within our company for others to say more. Before SD, I was the guy in the center of the room. Now, I am a bit hard to find, by design. If you walked into a management huddle at Hancock Lumber, it might take you a moment to pick out the CEO.

Thoughtfully doing less as CEO can be a liberating growth opportunity for others. The boss gets first dibs on the work of a company. I can decide when (or if) we will meet and what we will discuss. That's a powerful responsibility, not to be taken lightly. And while there will always be moments where decisive leadership is necessary, restraint is a deceptively effective leadership skill.

Holding the power but not using it is essential to the goal of dispersing power.

The truth is a collage of what everyone sees. It's the conformity of thought that kills alignment. Imagine a scene from a totalitarian regime rally in the great square before the imposing granite capital. The vote is unanimous, and the entire gathering chants in unison. That's not alignment. It's overreaching. It's intimidation and force, restricting the voices of others.

Self-centered organizations have often pursued a single truth recited by all. But that's not honest dialogue. In order for people to bare their souls, conversations must transcend judgment. Knowing what everyone thinks is a huge advantage for an organization. The quest for a single truth is an unworthy goal, for a more dogmatic time. Voices are unique by design. Conformity is overrated. True consensus comes from a diversity of views and a culture where everyone feels heard.

In order for people to say what they truly think, the culture of the organization must be safe. Specifically, the leaders must learn not to judge what people say. At Hancock Lumber, listening with restraint is one of the core leadership skills we are working to acquire. Group huddles, formed in circles—where the official leader is a bit hard to find—are our optimal communication venue. For authentic dialogue to take hold, the leaders must resist the temptation to respond to what everyone says, other than to thank each person for saying what they think.

In the age of shared leadership, we must learn to accept voices as they are. The only voice a leader should shape is his or her own.

* * *

THE FIRST NIGHT OF THE NSDA SYMPOSIUM is known as "Pass the Microphone Night." After dinner, everyone gathers to introduce themselves, sharing their own unique story. One by one the micro-phone is passed. Each voice, broken or weakened in its own unique way, takes their turn. Some people whisper; others wrestle with their words. A few just smile and have their spouse, friend, or seat neighbor introduce them.

Every once in a while a broken voice will suddenly fall back into form, and for a few sentences normalcy is restored. The speaker does not know when this will happen or why, but I've experienced it myself, and it always causes me to pause. *Hey, wait a minute; that's my original healthy voice. It still lives in there some-where.* Those moments are recognized by everyone in the room as they occur.

"The best part of having SD is that alcohol helps," someone says, holding the microphone.

The room erupts with laughter.

"It's true," I say quietly, nodding to the person beside me.

As the microphone reaches the back corner of the room, it arrives in Charlie Reavis's hands. Charlie is the CEO of the NSDA. He is a tall, thoughtful, and distinguished Southern gentleman with a successful background in the telecommunications industry. His words flow like a wave across the room, spreading optimism and responsibility to all.

"Think of yourself as the NSDA," Charlie says. "Each of you represents the NSDA in your local community. You are the one that creates awareness. You are the one that shares the story. You are the one that searches for answers, and a cure. You are the one that reaches out and builds your local support network. Without you, there is no organization. It's what you do that matters."

Charlie sees what nature knows. Power is dispersed, and every voice is unique by design.

His enthusiasm for his role reminds me of one of my favorite interviews between Bill Moyers and the great American mythologist, Joseph Campbell, recorded in 1988 as part of the documentary series *Joseph Campbell and the Power of Myth*.

Bill Moyers sits in one chair wearing a tan suit. His thoughtful eyes are rimmed by large glasses. Joseph Campbell sits beside him, looking very much the part of the distinguished yet lovable professor. He is wearing a tweed jacket, and his wavy hair has turned just the right amount of gray. Joseph's eyes are alive with knowledge, and the certainty that the idea he is sharing shall never become outdated.

Bill: You talk about something called the soul's high adventure. Can you explain what that means?

Joseph: My general formula for my students is *Follow Your Bliss*. I mean…find where it is [your bliss]…and don't be afraid to follow it.

Bill: Can my bliss be my life's love or my life's work? Is it my work or my life?

Joseph: Well, if the work that you are doing is the work that you chose to do because you love doing it, that's it. But if you think, oh gee, I couldn't do this or that…you know…well, that's your dragon that's locking you in.

Bill: Unlike the classical heroes, we're not going on our journey to save the world, but to save ourselves.

Joseph: And in doing that, you save the world. I mean, you do. The influence of a vital person vitalizes. There is no doubt about it. The world is a wasteland. People have the notion of saving the world by shifting it around and changing the rules and so forth… and no, that won't work…. Any world is a living world if it's alive… and the thing is to bring it to life…and the way to bring it to life is to find in your own case where your life is and be alive yourself, it seems to me.

* * *

LIFE IS ABOUT LOOKING INWARD and finding your own true voice and then releasing it to the world. Work should support, not thwart, this human calling. Work should be a place where people feel safe to turn inward and self-actualize. Imagine if everyone on Earth felt so secure in their environment that they could focus safely and honestly on their own truth, path, and personal growth.

We all come from a tribe, and its momentum pulls on us. Under duress it can feel safer to become preoccupied with what others should be doing. But spending too much time trying to change the world through others is to live in the "wasteland" of rearranging the rules that Joseph Campbell describes.

When we turn our focus inward and listen to our own voice, we enhance our ability to add value to the lives of others. It's like Joseph Campbell once said:

> And do you know who God is? It's you. All of these symbols in mythology refer to you. You can get stuck out there and think it's all out there.

* * *

THE ALLURE OF EXTERNAL DISTRACTIONS makes me think of Pine Ridge and its difficult journey back to economic independence. Before Western expansion, the Sioux tribes were self-sufficient. Today, nearly 150 years later, reservations like Pine Ridge are among the poorest and most government-dependent places in

America. How to break that spell is a question that often consumes me. It if were easy, it would have already been done.

Tribal sovereignty is one of the most common political phrases you will hear when the people of Pine Ridge discuss the future in their remote corner of the northern plains. The phrase has its origins in the Fort Laramie Treaties of 1851 and 1868 that acknowledged a nation-to-nation status between the Sioux tribes and the federal government. But what does *tribal sovereignty* mean today, and how is it best achieved? In the end, isn't *sovereignty* something all humans desire and aspire to pursue?

Although it will never be my role to lead this dialogue at Pine Ridge, I prefer the idea of *economic sovereignty* and the achievement of economic freedom from the federal government. There is no future in being dependent upon the center.

There is a deeply held sentiment at Pine Ridge that the federal government owes the tribe a significant modern-day commitment in exchange for the land that was taken, the treaties that were broken, the promises that were not honored, and the wrongs that were done. This perspective is 100 percent understandable. Perhaps never has America dealt more dishonorably than it did with the Plains tribes in the rush to claim the continent from "sea to shining sea."

But here is the big question: What if government can't ever fix what it broke? In fact, what if deeper federal engagement actually only perpetuates the existing dysfunctional patterns and makes things worse? What if expecting too much from government is a distraction that prevents the hard work of personal power creation from receiving the attention it deserves? I am always hesitant to ask these questions of my friends at Pine Ridge, but I can't stop thinking about them.

One subtle example of this dilemma can be found just a half-day's drive north of Pine Ridge on the Dakota Sioux Standing Rock Reservation. This traditionally disenfranchised community was once famous as the home of Sitting Bull. In 2016 the reservation again became a national story as tribal protests to halt construction of the Dakota Access Pipeline made headline news. In a tale reminiscent of David and Goliath, the tribe took on the pipeline and its parent company, Energy Transfer Partners, as well as the State of North Dakota, the Army Corps of Engineers, the federal government, and anyone else working on behalf of the pipeline's completion.

The $3.8 billion undertaking is designed to transport crude oil from North Dakota to an existing pipeline terminal in Illinois. Along the way, near the South Dakota border, the pipeline crosses under Lake Oahe, a section of the Missouri River dammed decades ago by the Army Corps of Engineers just north of the Standing Rock Reservation.

For its part, the pipeline company emphasizes that the Army Corps of Engineers held nearly four hundred public forums and met personally with dozens of Native tribes. The company and the Army Corps of Engineers maintain that numerous overtures were made to engage the Standing Rock Tribe in the planning process, but the tribe declined to participate. The company also stresses that there are eight other active oil pipelines already operating safely underneath Lake Oahe.

The tribe counters by stating that they were not consulted, their voice was not heard, and their water supply is being put at risk.

Both sides believe in their story. Both sides are sure they are right. Neither can acknowledge the other's position, so they fight. That's often how tribalism goes: everyone is talking, but no one is listening. Proving others wrong rarely creates progress.

Part of me was proud to watch the protest camp grow in the summer and fall of 2016. I knew a number of people from Pine Ridge who were there. To see the tribes use their voice stirred my soul. But still, part of me worried. What if the pipeline was a distraction in disguise for the people of Standing Rock and Pine Ridge—a way to keep them from the real work of rebuilding their communities from within? Although this idea made me feel uncomfortable, the question would not go away.

Over time, I came to feel disloyal about not asking the question. What if this is an important inquiry that should be given a voice, but I'm too afraid to ask? Diversity of thought is essential to a healthy community. The truth is hard to find, and it requires turning over rocks and pondering that which makes us uncomfortable. If I fail to ask the question, am I then just supporting the continuation of a broken pattern, externally focused?

What if the pipeline is not, in the end, a major threat to either the health or economic sovereignty of the Standing Rock Tribe? What if stopping the pipeline is not even environmentally healthy on a global scale? What if my authentic voice is here to put that question forth and I falter, instead staying silent?

Virtually everyone who lives on the Standing Rock Reservation consumes oil. The pictures of the protest site that appeared daily on television were filled with gas-guzzling pickup trucks and SUVs. It can't be that the people of Standing Rock just want to make sure that the oil they use passes through someone else's tribal lands. Are the pipelines in Russia and Venezuela (by way of example) environmentally safer or built and monitored to higher standards? What about the cost of transporting oil halfway around the world?

The United States is the world's largest consumer of oil. Approximately one in every five barrels of oil produced on Earth is digested here. The United States produces approximately nine billion barrels of oil per day and consumes about twenty billion barrels in return. Is that fair to the rest of the world, to consume double what we produce just because we can afford to buy it elsewhere? Shouldn't we bear the responsibility of producing our own share?

Despite these arguments, my biggest concern was still for the people of Standing Rock and Pine Ridge.

In a world where power is dispersed, we need to think differently about the mechanics of losing and regaining it. The government that broke treaties, confiscated tribal lands, and restricted Indian freedom generations ago cannot actually restore what was taken. If it could have made it right, it would have already done so long ago. Billions of dollars have been spent trying to fix the wrongs. But what if no amount of government intervention can set things right? What if too much focus on government (and what others need to do) only blocks attention from the indigenous truth—that the power you seek lives within you?

While it's not easy to let go of the past, releasing it may well be a prerequisite for attaining a self-directed future. The challenge reminds me of something that the writer and life coach Dan Sullivan once wrote: "The price for growth is to give up your grievances."

* * *

When you have SD, it becomes a bit easier to relate to any person or tribe who feels like they are not fully heard. At Hancock Lumber, I try to strengthen the voices of others—and not just because low levels of human engagement lead to lost opportunities for accuracy, productivity, and profitability. Work is not living up to its potential unless it adds more than just financial value to people's lives.

Everyone within an organization must learn to see the world with fresh eyes in order for the age of shared leadership to manifest. We each must find and release what my friend Christie Bates calls our "authentic self." Christie and I met at the SD conference in Nashville, where she presented a session on well-being through mindfulness. After her talk I made it a priority to track her down and introduce myself. Her ideas were compelling, and I wanted more.

"What does 'authentic self' mean to you, Christie?" I ask as we stand together in the back of the conference room during the afternoon break.

"*Authentic self* can be a difficult concept," Christie says. "I consider it more of a process or a path. To be one's authentic self is to be on a path that is leading you home. 'Home' for me is a life that is aligned with my values, and with what is mine to do and learn in this lifetime. When I am authentic, there is a sense of spontaneity, creativity, and service, and of moving in the direction of freedom from avoiding suffering. And yet, of course, there is the sense of 'me' that must do the choosing of thoughts, words, and actions that constantly correct deviations from that process and path.

"During your talk this morning you referred to the 'spark of divinity' that lives within each of us. In the moments of choice that fill my life, where there is a need to determine which direction is most authentically mine, I experience that spark of divinity as that which lets me know which direction leads me to freedom."

Work should be a place that enhances, not restricts, self-actualization. When you come into your authentic self, your ability to contribute to society grows. Hancock Lumber is strengthened when the people at the company find and share their voice.

The business of business is to help others self-actualize. Leaders that can self-actualize and then create a safe place for others to do the same are going to be the first to usher in the age of shared leadership.

* * *

LATER THAT EVENING, after the conference, I find myself standing outside the Grand Ole Opry with a ticket in hand. To my right, the sun is setting behind the Opry Mills mall, above the hard-charging Cumberland River.

You don't have to be a country music fan to get the chills at the Grand Ole Opry. As the show begins, I feel like I have come to some great mecca, a place of organic Americana that is so authentic it could only have evolved to its present form one performer and audience at a time. On this night old-timers like Bill Anderson and Bobby Osborne share the stage with new stars like Ashley Campbell and Brad Paisley.

"You don't pass over that spot on the floor without getting a chill," Bill Anderson says as he walks to center stage, where a circular section of the original Opry floor still resides.

After the show, across the street, I have a cold Dos Equis lager and chips and salsa before me. Suddenly, the guy on the bar chair to my left hits me in the shoulder and invites me to take a shot of Patron with him and his three buddies. Tattoos run the length of his fully exposed right arm. He is wearing a Detroit Tigers baseball cap as he tells a tale of transcending homelessness and surviving cancer. The room is loud, so I don't catch his name or the full story.

He doesn't need my name. He calls me *dude*.

I don't really like it when another guy calls me "dude," but I play along.

"Sure, what the heck—I'll have a shot with you," I reply.

"Dude, after a bout with cancer, the littlest shit means so much to you," he says, putting his hand on my shoulder and leaning even closer to me.

Moments later I'm presented with an oversized shot glass of Patron and a slice of lime. We salute the world and put down the Patron with one tilt of the hand and neck, each shaking our heads and making manly bar noises when we finish.

"What brings you here, dude?" he says.

Here is life's single greatest question, never fully answerable, but always worth contemplating.

"I spoke today at a voice disorder conference," I say, leaning in close so that he can hear me. Whenever there is a lot of background noise, my voice is a major challenge.

"I actually have the disorder myself," I say, pushing my words out into the crowded and noise bar.

"Dude, your voice sounds fine," he says. "Shit, I know lots of guys that I can't hardly ever understand. I understand you just fine."

Some time passes. He drinks. I drink.

"Dude," he says leaning back in toward me once again, "you don't actually know who I am, do you?"

By now we have spent the better part of an hour together. His question gives me pause. Who might he be? Is he someone famous, or is he just playing around? I can see both possibilities as I consider my response. A country singer? A NASCAR driver? Championship UFC fighter? Reality TV star? What makes someone famous in the world today is a discussion unto itself. And what does that even mean, to be famous?

Why is anyone famous on a planet that needs everyone to lead?

Uncertain how to reply, I use one of my favorite SD tricks and answer his question with a question. In the world of sales, we call it "reversing." All good salespeople know that the information they get is more important than the information they give.

"That's funny," I say. "I was about to ask you the same question. You don't actually know who I am, do you?"

He pauses, not expecting his question to boomerang back his way.

We both laugh, now equally unsure. We even do a little "bro hug" thing.

I love this scene. It's the perfect unexpected ending to a day spent searching for voices. In a world where every voice matters, what is fame, and who is truly famous anyway?

The truth is, we all are. We just haven't figured that out yet.

* * *

A FEW WEEKS LATER, I wake up under a warm multicolored quilt in cabin #14, the one dedicated to the legendary Hollywood cowboy Roy Rogers. A green wooden door separates two divided-light windows that face east onto the gravel parking lot. Images of Roy Rogers adorn the curtains and the light switches. The checkerboard carpet commemorates a bygone era. An old metal table with a single chair sits in the corner. The room is equipped with a fly swatter and a space heater. Both are necessary depending upon the time of year that you are here.

The Historic Log Cabins are located on the edge of town in Hot Springs, South Dakota, just off Route 87 as the road turns north and begins its climb toward Wind Cave National Park. It's my favorite place to stay in the Black Hills, and the owners, Steve and Jeanie, have become my friends.

As I step down into the bathroom, my head is within inches of the ceiling. I start the shower and the small mirror immediately fogs. I clear it gently with a towel, but the mirror still swivels and tilts on the wire behind it, so I relevel it when I'm done. There is beauty in the simplicity of my accommodations.

Shaving cream covers my face. A white towel, barely big enough to do the job, is around my waist. I wipe the mirror again and stare into my own foggy reflection. Water beads cling to the glass.

Who am I? What brings me here? These are questions that I have come to embrace, like an old friend, and it's moments of solitude in remote places such as this that best bring them forth.

These are timely questions at any stage of life, but it took a jolt for me to transcend the safety of my own externally focused narratives and take them on. My ability (and willingness) to look first and hardest at myself was initially triggered by an evolutionary astrology reading Deborah Dooley had done for me.

"Souls have multiple incarnations across time for the purpose of evolving," Deborah said.

That idea, unprovable as it was, intrigued me. If the essence of nature was evolution, then why wouldn't souls take that same journey? Even pretending it was true seemed healthy.

Three years later the housing and mortgage markets collapsed, and our industry jolted from comfort to chaos. I was then the forty-one-year-old CEO of our sixth-generation company. At the time, my self-identity was too intertwined with my role as the leader of our company.

The stress of protecting our company from the collapse of the housing and mortgage markets took a toll on me that I could neither see nor appreciate in the moment. I just remember working hard, doubling down on the intensity, and fighting through. Then, in 2010, at the peak of the economy's decline, I began to have trouble speaking. It took an entire year of visiting doctors and struggling to talk before I was diagnosed with spasmodic dysphonia. While no doctor can confirm this, I know it was the internalized stress of the first event that caused the second. I had so deeply identified with my role as CEO that I could not separate a shock to the business from a shock to my own existence.

When the smoke cleared, I needed a strange new land (Pine Ridge and the northern plains) where I could go and contemplate the meaning of the events that had transpired. Stripped of all external roles, who am I? Standing alone in the grasslands and timbered trails of Wind Cave National Park helps me contemplate my existence absent of any titles or organizational responsibilities.

We all have places that call to us. They whisper, and they do so for a reason. These are the places that help us find our voice.

Authenticity is often drawn out by courage born of crisis. I know this was true for me. It took the collapse of my industry and the subsequent partial loss of my voice to trigger an awakening. Look back at some of the most difficult moments in your own life. What brought you there, to the brink? What lessons were exposed? In what ways were you being invited to grow? The Universe does conspire to help us all, but the assistance often comes disguised as a problem. It can feel counterintuitive to realize that looking inward is most critical when the demands of the external world reach their zenith.

As I finish dressing, I am filled with anticipation. I am soon to depart for a day of hiking in the wilderness, and my senses are already on high alert.

Upon exiting the cabin I pause and lock the door with an actual key, the old-fashioned kind you will no longer find at a modern hotel. This key is gold, symbolic of the history of this timbered oasis on the northern plains, and it reminds me of the consequences of greed and overreaching.

As late as 1868 the Native tribes of the region were guaranteed this land forever through the Second Fort Laramie Treaty, which defined and updated the boundaries of the Great Sioux Reservation. The Oglala Holy Man, Black Elk, would later say that the sovereign agreement between the Sioux and the expanding American empire was meant to last forever, "as long as grass shall grow and water shall flow." But only six years would pass before General Custer would lead a military expedition (in violation of the treaty) across the Sioux reservation and make a much celebrated (or lamented) discovery. There was gold in the Black Hills.

The following summer, prospectors, settlers, and adventurers flooded the territory. The United States government made only a token effort to stop the invasion before demanding that the Sioux sell the Black Hills. When the tribes refused, the United States declared war. Many people vacationing in the Black Hills today, visiting places such as Mount Rushmore, likely do not realize how this land was so dubiously acquired. But if you are Sioux, or a member of another northern plains tribe, you remember. You have not forgotten, and your community has not yet recovered.

This is my twelfth trip to the Black Hills, the Pine Ridge Indian Reservation, and the sea of grass that surrounds them both. I keep expecting to reach a point where coming here feels redundant, less rich, and less meaningful. But that hasn't happened yet. If anything, the opposite has occurred. More trips allow me to go deeper.

When I am at Pine Ridge, I spend a lot of time with the people I know who live there. Many of them have become dear friends. But I also spend significant amounts of time alone, and this has become a ritual that helps me to listen, learn, and grow. I find myself in this place, using all the ingredients of a modern-day vision quest. In fact, I find us all here. Immersed in nature, I can grasp a glimpse of the connectivity that unites all living things. We are all related, and I can see and feel that in wild places like Wind Cave National Park.

In terms of genetic composition, each human being is biologically 99.9 percent similar to every other human being. It's disconcerting how much time and effort go into exploiting a 0.1 percent difference. The more we back up our perspective, the clearer the commonality that binds all living creatures becomes. Imagine, for example, looking at all that exists in the Universe from its theoretical edge. From that vantage point, all humans would look very much alike.

* * *

At 7:30 a.m. I arrive at the trailhead and park in the small gravel lot. The hike I have planned will take all day and will cover the last stretch of trail in this entire park that I have not walked. It's an accomplishment years in the making, but it took me a lifetime to arrive at this moment.

The sky is blue, the air is crisp, and every step makes a sound as I walk the dusty trail to the stream below, before ascending the nearest ridge onto the grasslands on the other side. As soon as I clear the ravine I see the buffalo. They see me as well. They are scattered and feeding. There are no trees nearby, so I will have to make my way carefully in order to get around them. My experience is that buffalo don't look for trouble, but they don't yield their ground either. I am attentive but calm. I have done all this before.

At certain spots along the trail I wait, unconstrained by time, for a large bull to drift by. I learned long ago that buffalo only move when it pleases them to do so. This suits me fine. I am in no hurry. In fact, escaping hurry is part of what brings me here. Moving at nature's pace has regenerative powers. There is a flow to nature, and I am already feeling a part of it.

As I walk along, my mind drifts. I think again about how nature disperses power. Everything I can see, smell, and hear is important and contributes to the health and balance of my surroundings. The sun, the wind, the grass, the insects, the birds, the groundhogs, the foxes, the deer, the elk, the buffalo, the trees, and the water all play an essential role. Even the beetles and the wildfires that kill the pine trees are necessary participants. Nothing here is without value. Everything I see has purpose. Every creature I come across has a voice. It's all connected. Separateness is an illusion.

For centuries, bureaucratic capitals have spun the tale that power lives out there, away from you. This orientation has significant implications. We are taught to look externally for strength and guidance.

Once again, I process these five short sentences in my head, and find myself actually whispering the words repetitively as I walk along.

Nothing here is without value.
Everything I see has purpose.
Every creature has a voice.
It's all connected.
Separateness is an illusion.

Depending on where you live in the modern world, it is easy to lose your sense of connectivity to the natural world. But this has consequences. The iconic Western image of man conquering nature in God's name is fraught with peril. Conversely, understanding our fundamental kinship with all the world's creatures has redemptive and rebalancing powers. Spending intentional time in wild places is a wonderful way to rekindle this knowledge.

The Lakota believe that everything that has ever lived comes from the same sacred energy source. As a result of this holy understanding, the Lakota would refer to the buffalo, deer, and elk as their "four-legged brothers." Killing an animal for food, clothing, tools, weapons, and shelter was no small matter. It was something one did with great reverence, prayer, and thanks. A small number of buffalo might give their lives so that the tribe might live.

The value of this philosophy transcends environmentalism and gets right to the heart of the opportunity to live and lead differently. After all, if everything that exists is connected, then all humans are related. We are not as different as our tribal dogma would have us believe, and this is simultaneously exciting and threatening.

Division is big business—perhaps the most powerful one on Earth. But we have become so accustomed to our tribal ways that we have normalized it all. Gender, race, age, ethnicity, religion, and geography are all excuses to divide. And each divide creates another empire. Every nation needs a government, every state a governor. Every religious institution needs a holy man, every race a protector and advocate. The politics, money, and power invested in division are almost incalculable, yet at times we barely notice, as it has become the normal state of affairs.

Imagine for a moment that the whole world came together as one unified village. While this has a charming allure, it also brings incalculable risk to the status quo. Countless positions of power would be compromised. Unity, despite its appeal, would topple too many castles, capitals, and empires. The entrenched bureaucracies and advocacy groups of the modern age are unwittingly threatened by the ancient wisdom that we are all related.

The realization that tribalism and division are moneymaking and power-taking exercises has not yet been confronted on a broad scale. Many will say that the races, religions, and nations of the world should overcome their differences and unite, but there is still too much influence to be grabbed in the politics of division. In addition, many of us still take a piece of our identity from being the outcast, from being misunderstood, from being the one who was exploited or left behind. Tribes provide identity and a sense of place. This makes transcending them a difficult proposition.

The problem with a preoccupation with external enemies is the opportunity cost of internal exploration. As long as there is an adversary "out there," we can postpone the real work of looking inward. Growth comes from within, but it's a hard lesson to learn, realizing that it isn't the other guy over there who needs to change.

At Hancock Lumber this understanding has altered the way I think about leadership. Progressive leadership is about working on oneself. It's about being the change. Today I encourage managers to spend less time supervising others and more time focused on their own growth. Self-awareness is essential to modern leadership. The biggest changes we can make always come from within. Leadership, it turns out, is an inside job.

But again, the culture of the organization must be safe in order for authenticity to thrive. When people feel judged, they become guarded. When an organization is led by ego, it fosters more ego.

I have found that talking openly about my own mistakes and weaknesses is helpful to me and others. It gives permission for authenticity. I have rarely seen a problem in our company that I could not trace back to me in some regard.

One of my favorite leadership exercises is to ask managers to identify a way in which they would like to see their team grow and change. Then, I simply ask each manager to focus on what they could do differently to facilitate that change. For example, if I would like to see the sales team spend more time prospecting for new clients, the action step is for me to become more disciplined in how I engage the sales team on the subject of business development. If I want our delivery drivers to take more pictures of the products they leave on construction sites, then I should be more consistent about commenting on the pictures as they are shared and inquiring about them when they are not. The idea is to identify something that frustrates you about what others are doing, or not doing. Then, look at yourself and identify how you might become the change. Looking in the wrong place for change is a common reason why the change we seek does not occur. The biggest opportunities for improvement always lie within.

We recently made some communication mistakes about a pending transition at one of our stores. I was pretty disappointed in our performance on the subject. But at the leadership huddle where the subject was discussed, I simply shared the list of mistakes I felt I had made. Without any further prompting, everyone else in the room then did the same.

✷ ✷ ✷

I was listening to KILI Radio (90.1 FM, The Voice of the Lakota Nation) just a few days ago on the reservation. I was driving back from a trip to the Badlands, returning to the Singing Horse Trading Post for dinner with my friend Rosie, who is the owner. My mind was wandering when some of the most encouraging words I had ever heard at Pine Ridge (or anywhere, for that matter) broke my trance.

"There is no way to get back to one hundred percent [pure Lakota blood] mathematically," the radio host explained in a distinctly Lakota accent. "The mixing of blood through marriage and childbirth is expanding, and there is no way back. When you play this trend out over the next fifty or one hundred years, well…we're all blending together. So we need to stop talking about Lakota pure blood. We need to broaden our vision of who we really are."

I remember thinking that the radio host was very brave. In a community that has so many valid reasons to look externally for blame and solutions, this thoughtful soul was asking his tribe to forgo that temptation and look inward.

"We have this romantic vision of who we are as a people," the speaker said. "But we are so far away from that vision today. [Riding] bareback, firing an arrow into a buffalo...we are so far away from that now. That's not who we are anymore. We need to embrace who we are today, not who our ancestors were generations ago."

Pine Ridge is a community that prides itself on its lineage. To confront the blurring and blending of bloodlines here was a bold act of consciousness. When it comes to tribal dogma, it takes intentionality to break through the veil. All cultures adopt an image of the world that aggrandizes their identity. Breaking this down takes courage. Deconstructing your own house is hard but necessary work.

Transformation of self is hard work, but waiting for government (or any other external source of power) to transform society is a fool's errand. It won't happen for two reasons. First, change comes from within, one soul at a time. No external forces can bring about the change you seek. Second, government gets its power from the divisions that exist in society, and ending those divisions would make the role of government very small. Governments derive their influence from their promises to protect you. They thrive off enemies. Any threat, real or imagined, will do.

∗ ∗ ∗

By now I have crossed the open grasslands and followed the trail as it disappears into the forest. The path before me twists and descends, dropping into a ravine. I can hear the river babbling below as it runs its course. There is a hot spring nearby, and I can smell the sulfur and see the steam.

At the bottom of the canyon I follow the river for some time before arriving at an intersection where my path turns right and climbs out of the shadows and back into the warm sunlight on the ridge above. I am sweating as I reach the top. My heartbeat has accelerated but my rhythm is strong, and I keep moving at a rapid pace. I have so much energy right now that I want to run, but I hold myself back, like a rider on a horse who knows the race is long. This is a place of vibrancy for me. It's a portal through which, at least for a moment, all the energy of the Universe can be mine. Nature is counting on me to be me, I think, as I glide forward through the wilderness. I am by now miles from the nearest road.

As I continue along my mind wanders back to the importance of self-awareness—the difficulty with which it is acquired, and the ease with which it can be lost.

I have spent several Halloweens at Pine Ridge, and the way the holiday is celebrated always intrigues me. Each year I listen to KILI Radio as community events are announced. Zombie-themed parades, costume parties, and dances are the most common activities. I have always contemplated the national popularity of zombie-genre television shows and movies with a bit of bewilderment. What's the attraction? Why are they so popular? They look stunningly boring and predictable to me. The zombie chases you but can never quite catch you. You lop off its head, and the zombie stumbles but then regroups and continues. That's the storyline every time. If you are being chased by zombies, you never quite lose and you never quite win. You can kill a thousand zombies in a day and be no better off tomorrow.

To be a zombie is to surrender your individuation and join the mindless horde. All the zombies move left, then right. You blend into the crowd, wearing the same tattered gray clothing as the zombie next to you. Your senses are dulled. You can lose an arm and feel no pain. It's a robotic state of semi-existence.

The current social infatuation with zombies is not without meaning. Zombies catch our attention because we are, on a subconscious level, afraid of becoming one.

It's the pull of our tribe, the routines we are born into, and the expectations that are placed upon us that combine to make finding our own true voice a difficult task. We are all born into a tribe. We grow up with the stories and dogma of that tribe. We get busy. We surrender. We follow along.

* * *

A FEW MONTHS AFTER THIS TRIP to the Black Hills I find myself Skyping once again with my friend Deborah Dooley from my office in Casco Village. Rain pelts the skylights above me in drum-like fashion, reminding me momentarily of Pine Ridge. As I face my laptop I see Deborah inside her home in the land of redwoods, north of San Francisco. She is sitting on her couch surrounded by blankets. Her white hair is pulled to one side, resting on her shoulder. Through Skype we transcend distance, sitting face-to-face although thousands of miles apart.

Which distance is real—the one that separates us or the one that connects us?

"You speak of zombies," Deborah says, as we chat like neighbors through our laptops, "which is just another reference point for the low end of human consciousness. There are five levels of consciousness, but the truth is, most people don't get very far.

Instead, the external world sabotages their growth. The early levels are all about conforming and adapting to an external authority. Adults, for example, who are stuck at level-two consciousness do not take consistent initiative for their own well-being and often see their situation as the fault or responsibility of others. It is not until people work their way to level three that they begin to take a step back and independently examine their own personal and tribal pathology."

Deborah pauses and adjusts her hair while I contemplate some of the key words and phrases she has just referenced. *Adapting to an external authority...stuck at level-two consciousness...independently examine their own pathology....*

"In what ways am I holding myself back?" Deborah asks. "In what ways is my community its own worst enemy? These critical, inward-looking questions pave the way for higher-level awareness. Level four is the goal—to come into your own personal power.

"When you have come into your own personal power, you suddenly recognize that everything in your life comes from your own choices, and from then on there is zero tolerance for any excuses or victimization. At level-four consciousness you begin to take one hundred percent responsibility for what's happening in your life. Level four is accountability-based consciousness. Here you learn to focus on yourself. You leave the world of tribalism and become an independent thinker, with your own voice. But this is very hard to do. Most people never reach level four; many live their entire lives in level two, focused instead on what other people need to do."

As I listen, I slide into my own classic trap of believing that I am gathering up sacred knowledge for the benefit of others, forgetting that I am the one who most needs to hear what Deborah is saying.

Deborah senses this and tosses me a wake-up call.

"In 2010 you were so merged with the fate of your company that the survival of the business became your personal survival. That chaos then manifested itself in your voice. You had vanished, fully submerged into your role as the CEO of the family business. Pain creates awakening. People will not change unless they have pain."

Deborah's words momentarily take my breath away. I look everywhere but at her before sitting up straight and making the inevitable eye contact she is waiting for.

"I know that's what happened," I confess, putting down my pen and giving the subject my full attention. "The company was a place for my ego to be served, and this external focus limited my self-awareness."

After auditing my breathing, my voice quality, and my body language to gauge the depth of my self-awareness, Deborah continues.

"Remember, Kevin—the majority of your planets sit in the twelfth house, which is ruled by Pisces. Pisces has no boundaries. It merges all the time; it fails to have an autonomous sense of self. That's what happened to you. That's what will continue to happen to you if you are not aware of what's going on inside you.

"You rely too much on your Botox," Deborah says. "Your voice is just a reflection of your habituated patterns. Your patterns of breathing and heart coherence all manifest themselves through your voice. Botox can't address the root causes of your disorder. You need to strengthen your own self-discipline and go deeper. You need to meditate. You need breathing exercises. You need to learn to keep your consciousness internally focused despite what is happening around you. You have to be willing to do the hard work. These are strong, deep patterns you are trying to break. Botox can't go where you need to go."

Once again Deborah has refocused me, on me. Writing a book is a dangerous exercise because you can easily convince yourself you are doing it for others. But I am the one who most needs to heed my learnings.

* * *

AT THE NEXT TRAIL-MARKER POST I sit down in a narrow meadow surrounded by pines and face the sun. I rustle through my green daypack and extract a bottle of water. I drink half of it right away and then stare into what remains. If you were a small insect floating inside this plastic container, you would know no other world beyond the boundaries of the bottle itself. Yet the barrier is actually transparent and thin, and beyond its confines exists a world so vast it could not possibly be imagined from within.

"What is the future of a reservation in the modern age?" I write in Evan's journal, before pausing and taking a bite out of a fresh green apple. Some juice from the apple squirts onto the page, partially blotting out the word *reservation*.

This planet has been carved up by humans into boundaries, surveyed and marked. But how real are they, and how long are they meant to last? Human boundaries are fluid by their very nature, like Aquarian energy itself.

I am reminded of this every time I leave South Dakota and drive west into Wyoming. Each time, without fail, I stop at the border crossing and take a picture of the big, bold sign that says WELCOME TO WYOMING. The letters are yellow, and below them is a silhouette of a cowboy, hat in hand, riding a bucking bronco beneath the Teton mountain range. On the bottom of the sign it reads FOREVER WEST. If I were to make a U-turn and travel back into my own tracks, I would immediately come to a smaller green sign that reads WELCOME TO SOUTH DAKOTA.

Invariably, when I cross this artificial construct of a border, there are no other human beings in sight. I am the only one here. Barbed wire and wooden fence posts drift off into the horizon as far as the eye can see, further dividing the land within each state. Not long ago, none of this existed here—no state lines, fences, or signs.

I don't think I was conscious of this habit for the first few years that I traveled west, but eventually it dawned on me that I always stop at these remote border crossings and take pictures. Why? What is it about these human boundary lines that fascinate me so? Whatever the source of this inspiration, my black Lenovo laptop now carries dozens of pictures of the signs that divide the northern plains.

As I stand beside my parked car on a lonesome stretch of highway at the point of another border crossing, I imagine the West as it once was, without borders or boundaries. I contemplate a band of Lakota Sioux moving west from the Black Hills toward the great buffalo hunting grounds near the Bighorn Mountains, along the tributaries of the Yellowstone River. Dust swirls as the entire village moves. Horses, dogs, tepees, children, warriors, grandmothers, and medicine men are all in motion. Suddenly, the caravan stops as the mobile village arrives at the WELCOME TO WYOMING sign. Curious looks and questions abound. What is this strange marker in a sea of grass? What does it mean? Why is it here in this particular spot? These signs that we consider normal would have been unimaginable just 150 years ago. We have gotten very good at constructing borders. Deconstructing them may prove harder.

* * *

As I CONTINUE DOWN THE TRAIL I realize that I haven't seen or heard another person all day. The birds are singing, and the wind is blowing through the pines. Up ahead in the distance I can see that the trees turn black. Tiny beetles have sent the cycle of this forest's life back to the beginning. Life creates death, and death creates life. It's a circle long celebrated by the Sioux.

Wisdom is a core value of the Sioux, who believe it can only be acquired through age, experience, and self-reflection.

One of my dearest friends from Pine Ridge is a Dakota elder, Catherine Grey Day. When I first began traveling to the reservation, she was living in half of a small trailer out behind the Singing Horse Trading Post. I remember one of our earliest visits together, during the year that we first met. We were upstairs having dinner at the wooden table between the kitchen and the bedroom where I stayed. There were four of us in all, and Catherine was describing the futility of measuring people by their bloodlines.

"There is a lot of jealousy here—lots of infighting, lots of distrust," Catherine said of Pine Ridge. "Who is more pure-blooded? I think people waste lots of energy on meaningless questions such as this. If we are all related, why does it matter who is truer-blooded?" Catherine was demonstrating what Deborah Dooley describes as level-three consciousness—the ability to stand back and begin to look critically at one's own self and tribe.

Another friend and elder from Pine Ridge, Verola Spider, shared similar sentiments with me one day as we sat downstairs in the trading post store where she was working. It was late on a Saturday afternoon, with less than an hour to go before closing time. There were no customers in the store, and the dream catchers hanging from the rafters swayed gently in the early evening air, pushed by the breeze through the open screen door.

"We are all related," Verola said in a steady, slow voice without looking up from her beadwork. "Some of us, the old, the real fluent speakers—we still believe that we are all related, and we try to teach that to our children." I could hear drums and chants from the small radio on the counter behind me. Otherwise it was quiet, and I waited patiently for Verola to proceed.

"When I am teaching in the classroom," Verola continued, "I try to teach my students that no matter what color a person is, we don't see the color. We see the spirit of the person, and then we know that we are all related. No matter where we come from, you always meet a person and it seems like you knew him for a long, long time. You don't look at the color of the person; you just know that you are related in some way. That means a lot. There are a lot of us who still believe that way, who still believe in the old ways. A lot of times you hear people saying, 'No, that's not the way,' but those people probably have a little bit of doubt in themselves. There are still a few of us left who believe in the old ways, who still believe that we are all related."

As I move forward I stop and touch everything I can reach. The bark is crisp. The seedlings are thick and flexible. The grass is soft. The rocks are smooth. The trail sweeps right and now walks the boundary line between old and new life. On one side, the trees are black and bare. On the other, the forest is thick with color and substance.

Eventually I emerge onto a familiar open expanse of grass. It is here that the trail I have just hiked for the first time intersects with an old trail I know well. Far out onto the buffalo flats a lone coyote stops and stares me down. I watch him through my binoculars. I recognize him; I've seen him before. He lives here and has seen me before as well. The coyote watches me without moving and then trots on. After a short time he stops again and turns my way. With a final glance he acknowledges and then releases me.

Time in the wilderness is one powerful way to strengthen our understanding of the connectivity we share with all living things. I once heard Catherine Grey Day describe her own family to me as a *wojopi*, which she translated to mean "a pudding that is all mixed up." She said her family is a collection of many tribes and races. I loved her explanation. Few people could describe something so delicate and complex in such a simple, playful way.

"So many people I know have mixed blood," Catherine once told me. "That's why it's so silly that we fight over which person is more pure blooded. We are all pretty much related when it comes right down to it."

What we do (or don't do) affects others. That's the essence of the Seventh Power.

We change the world by working on ourselves.

At the far edge of the grasslands the trail makes a final dive into the woods before emerging soon thereafter onto the empty road below. By now the sun is to my back and dropping in the sky. I have spent the day alone yet been with all the world.

Making ourselves whole on the inside is the pathway to unity on the outside. Leaders need to work first on themselves and become the change. Then leaders must create the cultural conditions that encourage others to do the same. For me it's about swapping ego for self-awareness. Work can become a place for self-exploration, but the conditions must be right.

Encouraging managers to supervise others less, and themselves more, turns the conventional view of leadership inside out. But it is the only path to deep change. We don't change others. We change ourselves, from the inside out. When leaders model this behavior, not only do they improve, but they also make it safe for others to follow.

Working on me is the best way to be of value to you. The chaos I see on the outside is but a reflection of the work I need to do within. Change, it turns out, must first be created from within.

This is the third essential lesson of the age of shared leadership.

CHAPTER 4

A Celebration of Soul

*"It's gonna take a lot of love to change the way
things are."*

—NICOLETTE LARSON

I can't remember what she said that made me cry....
We met for the first time less than forty-five minutes ago, and she doesn't even know my name. But here I am, sitting on bike #48, soaked in sweat, full of emotion and crying.

The tears reach their peak near the end of the class as the dance remix of "Amazing Grace" transitions without pause into U2's hit song, "Where the Streets Have No Name."

Maddy is at the front of the room on an elevated platform, and she's pumping hard now. This is the home stretch, and like a jockey on the last straightaway at Churchill Downs, she wants everything we have.

"Bring it home! Bring it home!" Maddy exclaims. The small microphone fastened to her right ear propels her words of encouragement to every corner of the dimly lit room. Beads of sweat roll off her face and trickle down her back. She's wearing a sports bra and spandex athletic pants cut above the calf. The wall behind her is one big mirror, and we can all see her from both sides as we pedal toward our own reflections. She's so fit and full of energy that it seems as if, just for a moment, all of humanity might be reborn.

Everyone is up off their bikes now, pedaling for speed from the standing position. It's only ten minutes past nine on Sunday morning, but this room full of aspiring warriors is sprinting hard. Pulsating lights break the darkness. Everyone is sweating…everyone is chanting…everyone is moving in unison. It feels like a modern-day sweat lodge. It's the sacred rite of the Sioux reinvented for twenty-first-century Boston. Across cultures and transcending epochs, humans have found rituals that release the sacred light that dwells within us all.

My twenty-four-year-old daughter, Abby, is three bikes to my left. She's the one who brought me here today. This is her favorite urban workout, and she raves about how refreshed she feels after each session.

As the music tails off, Maddy softens her tone. This is her closing sermon, the last message of the morning.

"Notice how you feel *now*, compared to when you started," Maddy whispers. Only moments ago she had been hard charging. Now her gentle, reflective energy flows throughout the room.

"Notice how you feel *now*, compared to when you started," Maddy repeats.

Calm…patient…powerful…confident…centered…loving… peaceful…alert…ready…fearless…. That's how I feel. These are the sensations that fill my mind, body, and soul.

We dismount and stand on the right side of our yellow bikes for a final group stretch and shared prayer. Following Maddy's lead, we all reach our arms out and then up, in a circular motion, toward the sky. We bring our hands together and lower them slowly, halting at our heart in the *namaste* position. This gesture represents the understanding that a divine spirit dwells within us all. It's the k'é of the Navajo in a different language.

The Seventh Power, I think. It lives within us all. *Namaste.*

"May you be joyful, loving, and, above all else, fearless," Maddy says as the room shares a deep breath and a final, slow exhalation. With that she turns on the lights.

It is Sunday morning at SoulCycle, near Copley Square, and I've just been to Boston's newest church.

* * *

As I exit the studio, the towering glass edifice of the John Hancock Building reflects the clear image of a passenger jet accelerating away from Logan Airport. A gentle breeze pushes the summer air toward the Charles River, past rows of red flowers that line Clarendon Street.

"How'd you like it, Dad?" Abby asks, joining me curbside.

"Oh, my goodness, Abby, I loved it! Thank you so much for bringing me. I'm already hooked!" I say, still dripping with sweat.

We high-five and then cross the street toward Copley Square and the Trinity Church. Steam rises from a nearby manhole cover, bringing the distinct scent of the city's underground with it. The church itself is encircled in scaffolding, and a construction barrier surrounds the perimeter. A banner halfway down the fence line flaps in the breeze. On it is a picture of two happy angels wearing yellow safety hard hats with a caption that reads "God at work."

This historic church is a puzzle of towers, crosses, gargoyles, stained glass, and stone. The 7:45 a.m. Holy Eucharist has ended, but the 10:00 a.m. service has not yet begun. It's a rare moment of Sunday morning solitude for what is perhaps the most famous place of worship in all of Boston.

Trinity Church is the flagship of the Episcopal Diocese of Massachusetts. The church was founded in 1733 (before any of Crazy Horse's ancestors would have ever met a white man) and boasts a modern congregation that numbers in the thousands. The church is also the temporary place of worship for tens of thousands of visitors to Boston each year.

SoulCycle, founded in 2006 in New York, is a chronological toddler when compared to this nearly three hundred-year-old New World monument of Christianity. Yet today in Boston they share the same street corner and, arguably, a complementary mission. Founded on a shared vision that a contemporary fitness class could be much more than just a physical workout, Elizabeth Cutler and Julie Rice opened their first studio in Manhattan. The experience they designed became so popular that by 2012 (the same year I began traveling to Pine Ridge), SoulCycle had reached the West Coast.

The upstart SoulCycle and the titan that is the Trinity Church are both houses of guided spiritual exploration in a world that is rapidly expanding its offerings for those who wish to seek, find, and share their own true voice.

May you be joyful, loving, and, above all else, fearless. Maddy's parting words come back to me as we cross Dartmouth Street in front of the Boston Public Library. Pigeons scatter as we arrive at the sidewalk on the other side.

What is it about pigeons and public libraries? I muse, momentarily distracted.

SoulCycle has left me feeling renewed, as if I am floating, like the sensation that sometimes comes my way in the backcountry of Wind Cave National Park or on the bluffs above the Singing Horse Trading Post at Pine Ridge.

Above all else, fearless...

I went on my own vision quest several years ago, deep in the Black Hills. At the conclusion of that long day of wandering in the wilderness, a single sensation rose above all others: I had lost my fear—at least momentarily.

That afternoon I tasted what it felt like to let go of fear—to let it simply drift away. I understood that the sensation was likely not permanent, but it didn't matter. At that moment, nothing scared me, and a deep sense of calm filled my body. I was not in a hurry, nor was I late. I had no destination, nor was I lost. I had not succeeded, nor had I failed. I was just there, being, in the moment. Judgment and worry vanished; fear dissipated.

What was I afraid of to begin with? I asked myself later that evening in the corner booth at the dimly lit Pizza Hut in Hot Springs, just south of the park. Was my fear driven by the responsibility I felt to take care of others? Was it a fear of not fulfilling the expectations I carried with me? Was it a fear of not living in alignment with my own true voice? Or was it simply the universal experience of being human? Whatever it was, it had temporarily vaporized.

We need institutions in our lives that remind us that the answers to life's deepest questions live within us. SoulCycle is a place where the Seventh Power is honored, nurtured, and encouraged. At SoulCycle, each individual rider—not the corporation itself—is the power source of the company. If enough riders have exceptional experiences, the company will thrive as an outcome. But the experience must be multifaceted. It can't just be physical any more than work in the twenty-first century can be just about a paycheck. The "soul" in SoulCycle is the secret sauce. Anyone can get a workout.

Why not make the authentic self-expression of the human spirit the focus of business? People excel when they come into their own true voice and feel free to be exactly who they are. By energizing and encouraging individuals, corporations can not only achieve business success, but they can also change the world. A heightened sense of self-worth is transformative.

For centuries the world of work and the world of spirituality have been separated. By "spiritual" in this context, I mean learning, growing, and blossoming on the inside. People typically worked on weekdays and went to church on Sunday. Workers sacrificed during the week in order to live more fully on the weekends, on vacations, and in retirement. But why? In the twenty-first century, this trade-off is neither necessary nor optimal. Globally, engagement levels are exceptionally low. This is so for one reason. The experience of those who work has not yet become a big enough priority at work. Putting more personal meaning into work for each worker seems like such a timely way to reposition the very nature of work itself.

I am talking about something more here than simply valuing employees. Virtually all companies value their employees. But in the traditional context, employees are appreciated and recognized for what they do for the company. The focus almost always comes back to the company.

Imagine flipping that script. Imagine valuing employees first as amazing human beings, who, because they are amazing, will do great things for the company. It's a subtle but significant transformation in thinking. The company is a platform for individual growth and self-exploration. The company is a place where humans can join teams, express themselves authentically, and find their voice. The company becomes a safe zone for individuals to come into their own power and then go forth and change the world. The company will benefit, but that benefit is a by-product of celebrating the human spirit.

The idea is to make the employees, not the company, the center of attention. It's a philosophical and literal proposition that results in the shrinking of the ego of the corporate center.

Ironically, in this model, the company itself can achieve even greater success. Everyone who works understands the importance of the organization as a whole. Everyone who works already knows they are there to serve, protect, and advance the company. That idea is already broadly understood. In any event, loyalty to the corporation will increase as people feel authentically heard and celebrated.

In the old days of church and state building, the objective was to make the capital as grand and as imposing as possible. The federal buildings in Washington, DC, are a marble and granite ode to grandeur, a testament to the idea of an imposing headquarters— towering and sprawling above the populace—guiding and protecting us all.

In the age that is dawning, the individual will increasingly become the center of attention and the capital will be harder to find. SoulCycle understands this. The company is all about the individual soul, of an individual rider, on a bike that goes nowhere.

Personal freedom enhances organizational engagement. Think back to your days in school. Remember that special teacher who understood you on a personal level and encouraged you to trust your voice. How did you feel about that class? Chances are, you loved it. Chances are, you excelled. When we feel heard, understood, and valued as we are, we are much more likely to be highly engaged.

Humanity has experienced centuries of organization-centric thinking. This orientation is so ingrained that it's hard to see. But we are entering an age where individuals are coming into their own power. This is why engagement is so low and upheaval so prevalent. People are looking for deeper meaning and more spiritual value from the organizations they serve. Organizations have simply, so far, been slow to adjust.

This budding social transformation does not mean that organizations will dissolve; it simply means they must reorient. In the new model, a company can thrive by helping its employees to thrive. The purpose of the company is to serve the individuals who work there. Companies that do this will be rewarded by record levels of employee engagement and care for the organization in return. Pushing power out, away from the center, is the new path to excellence.

This may seem like a big change, but it's really not. A slight adjustment to our corporate vision is all that is required.

Take the simple example of being on time. When our mills start running in the morning, every position is critical. If one person is missing, every other person is affected. But instead of preaching from above about attendance and the importance of Hancock Lumber's production goals, we create the space in huddles for each individual to talk about how their experience is impacted when someone is unexpectedly absent. The realization is that you aren't just showing up to serve the company; you are showing up to serve the human beings beside you.

Even a lumber company must learn to serve a spiritual purpose.

Again, what do I mean by *spiritual* in this context? I mean, beyond monetary. Work should matter—on the inside, in a very personal way—for everyone who does it. Work should help people come more fully into their own identity. Self-actualization is a sacred and holy act because we are bringing our unique voice forth and sharing it with the world. Work is one of the best potential social platforms for this to occur. That's what I mean by *spiritual*.

Company goals (such as profitability or revenue growth) are no longer an end in and of themselves, but rather something that is manifested as a result of serving others. Improving people's lives by helping them find their own voice becomes the organization's mission. When this happens, the company itself can soar on the wings of the exceptional performance of an inspired team. The individual, not the capital, is the new power source.

When we share messages around the company about our core values, it is typically frontline employees describing what the company means to them, in their own words. Rarely would you see me on the company's internal communications network explaining what we are all about. Since we have 525 employees, we have 525 iterations of who we are. Each voice is an authentic representation of Hancock Lumber in the present moment. The company is the sum total of the individuals who compose it. We serve the company by serving each individual who works there.

Organizational success in the modern age depends upon real value creation for others—as defined by others. Pandering, or just saying what people want to hear, adds no value. Likewise, spinning tales of dogma and fear to keep your tribal circle tight is counterproductive. Tribal membership is increasingly becoming voluntary. No one is bound for long anymore to their family, their school, their place of worship, their job, or even their government. The expansion of mobility is a hallmark of the modern age. Increasingly, people keep moving until they find the places that serve, strengthen, and honor them.

* * *

A WEEK AFTER MY VISIT TO BOSTON I'm standing on the concrete floor inside our Casco mill. The entire crew is either sitting on blue wooden benches in front of me or standing near the yellow safety rails that surround the perimeter of the manufacturing line. Red hard hats with the Hancock Lumber logo are everywhere.

Apart from the sound of my own voice, this long, wood-framed building is unusually quiet. Normally at this hour you would hear the high-pitched rhythm of the planer and the rattling churn of the wood-waste chipper in the background. Here, everyone is typically in motion.

But right now the entire team is still, and thinking. It's the end of our quarterly huddle, and much of the talk has concerned safety initiatives, quality control, and productivity performance. Now it's my turn to share a few words, and today I'm after something even more important: human engagement, and the value of meaningful work.

"We work for financial reasons, but we also work to belong to something larger than ourselves," I say to the group. "A company needs to be a place where people feel valued and heard. It's not enough just to be profitable or earn a paycheck. Work needs to also add nonfinancial value to people's lives. We want this company to be a place where everybody leads and can feel their own worth and value. Thank you for answering that call and taking so much pride in what you do."

After my short talk, I lean on the rail and listen to the next person speak. Safety awards are being given out. The facility has gone over a year without a single work restriction from injury, and we were recently certified by OSHA's Safety and Health Achievement

Recognition Program (SHARP), its highest national safety award for manufacturers. Safety results at that level can only be achieved when each person on the team is a leader.

Unemployment in Maine is currently at a forty-year low. Many companies, both locally and nationally, are struggling to fully staff their organizations, but we aren't. Of the 525 positions at Hancock Lumber, only two are currently open.

What created this?

The key for us was simply resetting the mission. We decided to make the people who work at Hancock Lumber the top priority of Hancock Lumber. Learning to see the hearts of employees as the power source of a company creates a whole new set of possibilities.

I have listened to lots of executives talk about aging demographic trends, low unemployment rates, and the difficulty of hiring enough people to do the work of the company. For me, that's an external view of an internal problem. Maine has hundreds of thousands of people who work. At Hancock Lumber, we only have room for a tiny fraction of the state's working population on our team. In any economic cycle, the key is to focus on the micro environment inside our company, not the macro economic conditions beyond our reach or control. Small is the new big.

At Hancock Lumber, we grow trees, but that is not our core objective. We make lumber, but that is not our primary purpose. We manage logistics, but that's not our most important task. Our one big goal is to add value to the lives of the people who work at Hancock Lumber. Work should add more than just economic value to the lives of the people who do it.

There is a quote that lives at the bottom of every email I send. It's from British author and marketing consultant Simon Sinek, and reads: *Customers will never love a company until employees the employees love it first.*

An organization's true value is not defined by its revenue growth or profitability. While those are important metrics for our business, they are outcomes of a higher purpose. The mission is to add value to people's lives. Profitability, productivity growth, and exceptionally high levels of customer satisfaction are important, but they are outcomes of a bigger social goal.

Where in the modern world can adults grow? Lots of places, I suppose, but work can become the leading venue. In America there are 160 million people who work. Globally, there are two billion workers. The average full-time worker in America devotes forty-eight hours a week to their job. Careers last for decades. The time and energy humans invest in work cannot be just an economic proposition. As traditional institutions like centralized governments struggle around the globe for effectiveness, work can become the new incubator of societal change and human progress. Self-worth is the fuel that can change the world. Work can be a place where everyone can see their value, find their voice, and grow.

But for this to happen, business leaders must learn to think differently about their roles, and the very mission of a corporation must evolve.

SoulCycle is built around the fundamental proposition of improving the lives of their riders.

Take Your Journey
Change Your Body
Find Your Soul

SoulCycle knows that if the company adds value to the lives of others, it will be rewarded and successful in return. But the focus must be on people, not customers or employees. When I see someone shine within our company, I do not see a great "worker"; I see a great *person*.

* * *

THE FOLLOWING MONTH I AM HEADED once again for SoulCycle, this time with my daughter Sydney. Even though it's late July, it feels like October. The wind is blowing the rain sideways as we walk with our heads down beneath two cheap umbrellas that constantly threaten to collapse on us. Puddles grow in size at each street corner as passing cars send water careening our way. But we laugh as we go, undeterred.

Eventually, mercifully, we reach SoulCycle, step inside, and shake ourselves off. With just a few minutes to spare, we get locked into our pedals and ready to go. Sydney is two bikes away to my left, looking fit and strong, like she could lead the class herself. My legs turn slowly during the warm-up and my heart beats in anticipation of what's to come.

Erin, today's instructor, is busy up front, prepping her music, adjusting the lights, and checking on her bike under the spotlight on the elevated podium. At exactly 4:30 p.m. the two white doors at opposite ends close, the room goes dark, and Erin welcomes us to the sacred space that is the SoulCycle studio.

"We had a company-wide conference call today," Erin says, mounting her bike. "The theme of that call was integrity. As we grow as a company, we need to remember the essence of who we are. We need to stay true to our core values. This is important for each of us as individuals, as well. We each need awareness into the essence of who we uniquely are. Integrity is staying true to your own voice. Let's keep that idea in our hearts today. OK! Let's ride!"

Honoring the individual is the new path to organizational effectiveness. After centuries of centralization, it's time to localize once again. It's not coincidental that society's biggest institutions, such as government and organized religion, are struggling to retain membership, member confidence, and overall effectiveness. The momentum has shifted in the balance between centrally scripted narratives and the localized search for meaning and personal truth. The individual, not the capital, is the new power source.

Every wheel in the room springs into motion as the music begins. A few minutes later we are all out of the saddle, churning from the standing position and going for broke, pedaling in the dark on a bike that goes nowhere.

"Let's make integrity the theme of this ride," Erin suggests. "Pedal with integrity. Don't take a rotation off. Make each turn of the wheel count."

Erin goes quiet and dives back into her bike. Music and spinning wheels are now the only noise.

For the next forty-five minutes a room full of strangers synchronizes itself behind a hard-charging young woman on the elevated bike.

"Energy is real," Erin proclaims. "Feel the energy around you. Merge with it. Release the energy that doesn't serve you. Breathe in and absorb the energy that does. The energy you bring into this room matters. It's the energy you share. Be intentional about the energy you let into your life!"

At the end, as the wheels drift to a stop, riders dismount feeling refreshed, re-centered, and reborn. I am so wet with sweat that my T-shirt clings to my body.

At my locker, I look up at the messaging on the bright, white wall:

Addicted, obsessed, and unnaturally attached to our bikes,
high on sweat and the hum of the wheel.

* * *

THE AWARD-WINNING WRITER Thomas Friedman is one of the first modern thinkers to identify the flattening of the world as a term to describe the expanding capability we all share to connect globally with other individuals and build our own tribes. Distance as a barrier is dissolving before our eyes. Once upon a time emperors decided what the truth would be, and it was then written and handed down. Today, individuals are increasingly defining their own truth and creating their own networks for thinking and collaboration. Transportation, information, and communication technology have rewritten the rules of human engagement. Governments, religious institutions, schools, and corporations are no longer the sole gatekeepers of truth building. Today we are each invited to be the emperor of our world, determining when and where to join forces and build alliances.

When I was a child, growing up on a quiet country road in Casco, Maine, halfway between the town dump and the village, we had four television stations to choose from, and we tuned in by turning a dial by hand. *Newsweek*, *Time*, and *Sports Illustrated* showed up at our house once a week. The first time I saw a cable TV show was during my sophomore year in college, and using a satellite from space for my personal benefit was still years away. I called home from the pay phone on the second floor of my fraternity house once a week. Every Sunday we would all form a line, sitting on the floor in the hall, waiting for our turn to use the only phone in the building.

While humanity's challenges remain formidable, we may take for granted how much society has progressed in ways that benefit everyone. Power is shifting from groups to individuals. If you don't like your church, you can find a new one. If you don't feel inspired by your job, you can change it. The individual is gaining mobility and exercising free choice. Companies that recognize and honor this inevitable trajectory are going to have a big advantage over those who think the center is the source of power.

This explains what brings me to the Thinking Cup coffee shop at 85 Newbury Street in Boston on another unusually cool morning in July. It is 7:30 a.m., and I'm waiting for Maddy, the SoulCycle instructor from the first class I took. Having now been to Soul-Cycle several times, I am struck by the freedom each instructor has to speak with their own voice and design their own classes. In this way, each individual instructor is creating and designing the company in real time. Riders are free to follow the instructors who most inspire them.

Maddy comes down the stairs wearing full-length gray spandex pants, a fleece pullover, and low-cut black sneakers. A backpack rests on her left shoulder, and her blonde hair is pulled back. She has just finished a class.

"Hello," I say. "Thanks for making the time to see me."

"I'm intrigued by your interest in SoulCycle," Maddy replies.

"What brought you to SoulCycle?" I ask Maddy over juice and a breakfast sandwich.

"Well, it just kind of happened," Maddy says. "I was trying to follow my heart more and more, and there was just something about the organization and its mission that pulled me in."

Twenty-eight years old, raised in Rhode Island, Maddy recently returned from eight years of living in Los Angeles.

"I was working in the entertainment industry when I heard about this new cycling class," Maddy recalls. "I didn't have a ton of money at the time, but I would save a little each week to go to the classes. Eventually people there began watching me, and they were like, 'Maddy, you're perfect for this. You should look into becoming an instructor.' Pretty soon I was off to New York City for training. That's where it all started for me. Going from LA to New York was a lot, though. I didn't like the subway, so I walked everywhere—like, twelve miles a day, plus classes."

"What do you like most about being a SoulCycle instructor?" I ask.

"I love to be of service to others," Maddy says, her eyes lighting up. "I like seeing how the work I do can provide this little spark in people. I like that what I do can make a difference in the lives of others."

"Why do you think SoulCycle has such an impact on how people feel?" I ask. "What is it exactly that sends people away from a class feeling as if they were reborn?"

"SoulCycle is a place where people feel safe, even encouraged, to pour out their emotions. This is cleansing. SoulCycle gets at the stuff we all keep inside. It needs an outlet," Maddy says.

"Yes," I say. "We are all here on Earth just trying to find our own voice and release the best of who we are. I think organizations that understand this, like SoulCycle, are leading us forward."

Maddy's eyes widen, and she nods her head. "All that stuff we keep inside...it needs a place to empty itself on a regular basis," Maddy says. "SoulCycle provides that opportunity for people to cleanse themselves from the inside. You see the sweat on the outside, but it's the work we do on the inside that makes the difference."

She pauses.

"There is a level of vulnerability that our classes intentionally expose. The room is dark; the music is inspiring; you are pushing yourself hard on the bike. You are there, serving yourself, surrounded by others who are doing the same. I think it all combines to give our riders permission to be vulnerable. Is SoulCycle a physical experience? Yes, of course. But lots of fitness companies offer a physical experience. SoulCycle goes beyond that. It's an emotional and spiritual experience too."

"Why do you think people conceal their vulnerability in their daily lives?" I ask. "Why does it take a place like SoulCycle to help people release what's bundled up inside us all?"

Maddy rocks gently as she sits with her legs crossed beneath her in the chair.

"I think it's fear," she says. "Fear is what innately drives pretty much everything. Being able to manage the fear within you is the thing. It's like, we either turn our fear into fuel or we just collapse from it. If we don't release our fear, we are overcome by it. SoulCycle is a safe place where people can get at their fear and overcome it."

This company is thriving on the premise of self-exploration and self-actualization. We are drawn to people and places that accept us as we are and encourage authenticity.

"What's that energy like?" I ask. "At the peak of the best class experiences, what does it feel like? I've felt it myself, so I know it's real. When the energy of all the riders combines, you can feel it in the room. But I'd like to know how *you* would describe it. What does it feel like to you, as the instructor, leading the charge?"

"That peak energy in class is the highest high you could ever feel," Maddy responds, her face lit up. "It's shared energy. It's otherworldly. Chasing the perfect momentum and becoming part of a collective energy in a class—that's what keeps us coming back as instructors. A lot of us have performance backgrounds. It's like theater, or being onstage, and really going after the energy of the audience. It's that same rush. We don't do anything alone in there. Everyone in the room creates the energy at its peak, and when we hit that high, together, everyone moving in unison, sweating, pouring it out—it's magical."

That's the Seventh Power at work. The instructor facilitates the class, but the entire group, together, creates the energy.

"Tell me about the 'soul' in SoulCycle," I ask.

"The soul in SoulCycle is everything. You could go anywhere and ride a bike. It's the spiritual experience that makes our program different."

You could go anywhere and ride a bike. That's so true for all organizations. *You could go anywhere to buy lumber,* I think. What distinguishes organizations? It's the soul they have, and the authenticity with which they share it.

You have to look beneath the surface to find the real mission of a company. Lumber, for us, is a platform for a higher purpose. The purpose of the company is to add value to the lives of the people who work there. Of course, we are going to be highly engaged in the process of making exceptional lumber efficiently, but that's not the reason we exist. Organizations exist to improve the lives of the people who belong to them.

"Despite all the emotional energy we, as instructors, put into encouraging others, I still realize that I have to focus on myself, my own preparation and performance, most of all," Maddy says. "It's all about being a disciplined student yourself. You can't lose that hunger to keep expanding, learning, and growing. You have to work hardest on yourself."

Maddy unbundles her crossed legs and lets them fall back to the floor. She is calm and visibly centered.

"When you think about it, how could anyone possibly help others to find their peaceful, centered self without first achieving that state for one's self?" I reply. "We are each here to work on ourselves. When we make ourselves stronger, we become more valuable to others. But it all starts within us. The world is changed from within."

"I grew up Catholic," Maddy tells me, "and it was very disciplined. Not bad; just regimented. As an adult, I like finding my own truth. You know—taking nuggets from the world around you, little things that strike you positively, and turning them into your own. Other things that come your way that aren't so helpful, you try to just let them go. It's like—what actually fits me, and what doesn't fit me...that's life, isn't it? Learning to pick and choose what you want to put in your own life. It's all about knowing who you are and being true to it."

"Under the old bureaucratic order, the truth was often something that was given to you from above, and memorized," I say.

My voice is tight and strained, but I am inspired by our conversation and press on.

"You know—it was the head of the household, the teacher in front of the classroom, the spiritual leader of the church, the CEO, and the heads of state. They stood on the podium and handed down the carefully scripted rules.

"But the new age—well, that's going to be different. The new age is going to be more about helping others to find their own voice. Organizations that get this are going to thrive. The new path to progress requires deconstructing bureaucracies and making the headquarters smaller. But that's tough to do. If you are in the center, you want to hold on to what's there, or even expand your control. But the truth is that someone closer to the source has a better feel for the nuances of the local conditions than you do. Pretend, for example, that you are leading the Department of Education in Washington, DC. How could you possibly know best what a unique fourth grader in Maine needs this week? It's bulky, trying to lead from the center. Local flexibility and broadly dispersed responsibility are the new power sources. That's what I find so endearing about your organization."

"That's us," Maddy replies with a smile. "I'm so glad you can see that. It's reaffirming. It makes me feel good about the mission we are on, and the work we do. I believe in it. You have to believe in the work you do; otherwise…well, it's just work."

* * *

THE FOLLOWING DAY I AM SITTING at the Parish Café, facing Tremont Street in Boston's South End. Erin Lindsay, another Soul-Cycle studio star, sits opposite me across a small wooden table. Between us sits a giant meatball, a hummus plate, and two sparkling waters.

Erin, twenty-nine years old, looks every bit the part of the rockstar SoulCycle instructor. She has just finished her third class of the day. Her hair is pulled back in a wet bun underneath a brown baseball cap with the word SOUL across the front, in large letters. She is wearing low-cut canvas Converse sneakers with no socks, a tan skirt, and a gray sleeveless athletic top that subtly reveals a variety of tattoos.

Erin grew up in West Bloomfield, Michigan. Her life goals began to form when she was just six years old and her dad took her to the historic Fox Theater in Detroit to see the Radio City Rockettes.

"I knew then and there that I wanted to be one," Erin says.

After high school, Erin went to college in New York City on a dance scholarship and soon thereafter began auditioning for the Rockettes.

For six consecutive years, Erin auditioned. For six consecutive years, she didn't receive a call. But then Erin did something most people would not have the fortitude to do: she went back a seventh time and auditioned again.

"My dad taught me never to give up," she says reflectively.

After the seventh audition Erin got the call she had dreamed of: she was a Rockette.

"That's how I learned that your auditions in life start when you walk through the door. No, actually, I learned that auditions start when you wake up in the morning. What kind of thoughts are you going to have? What kind of energy are you going to bring? That's where your audition truly starts."

Each spring, like all the other dancers, Erin was required to try out again. Being a Rockette is like being a New England Patriot: you have to make the squad every year. But after six seasons, her Rockette career was over.

That spring Erin was bartending in New York City (waiting for the phone call that never came) when a friend asked if she wanted to check out the new cycling class that everyone was talking about.

"Endings are beginnings," Erin says. "Missing out on the Rockettes that year turned into one of the best things that ever happened to me. That's what brought me to SoulCycle."

After just one class Erin was invited to audition to become an instructor in the company's basement studio in the West Village.

"I think our future bumps into us all the time, but we're often too busy, or too distracted, to notice," I say.

Erin nods.

"It's rigorous," she adds, referring to becoming a SoulCycle instructor. "You think you're tough, but the process tests you. SoulCycle is all about hiring instructors with a visible thirst for life and a passion for storytelling through music—a perfect fit for me, but I had to work for it."

By 2014 Erin had done so well that she was part of the original SoulCycle team sent from New York to open the Boston studios.

"Only two of us who started things in Boston are still here," Erin says with pride. "I still get nervous before teaching, though; every class is a big deal to me. I love my job. Every class is an opportunity for self-expression, connecting with riders on a soul's level. It's art—plus a kick-ass workout. I mean, a great class will touch on pretty much every single emotion you have."

Erin is refined yet edgy. I like her style. She has her own voice.

"When they trained us, we were taught *not* to leave our baggage at the door," Erin continues. "You know, in much of our culture we are taught the opposite—to leave our baggage at the door, to keep it hidden and out of sight. But that's not who we are at SoulCycle. The whole point of SoulCycle is to bring your baggage with you into the room and work it out on the bike."

"Hiding the baggage is counterproductive," I say. "Leaders play a big role in creating an atmosphere where this can happen. If leaders are vulnerable, they make it safe for others to be vulnerable."

I'm inspired, ready to ride all over again.

"SoulCycle is special because of the authentic opportunity we create for self-expression," Erin says. "I want my riders to have a breakthrough on the bike, emotionally *and* physically. That's the most important thing to me—more important than hitting the perfect rhythm."

Erin pauses before resuming.

"Each rider takes a similar physical journey, but they take their own individual emotional journey. In the early days in New York City people would fire their therapists after starting SoulCycle, because they made more inner progress in forty-five minutes on that bike than they ever, ever made in their therapists' offices.

They helped themselves right there on that yellow bike that goes nowhere. It's pretty fuckin' awesome, actually.

"Slowing people's minds down…that's what I love doing," Erin says. "Finding the right pockets in the music and knowing what to say—that's the art of it all. It's all about coming into your own identity up there on the bike. As an instructor, when you can finally shake the nerves and just close your eyes in front of fifty people and rock it—you know, be yourself fully, own who you are—that's the best feeling."

"Humanity is calling out for a fresh approach to leadership, one that disperses power and strengthens the voices of others," I say. "SoulCycle is an early adaptor, ahead of its time, mentoring people on a new path."

"Thank you," Erin says, sitting tall and confident. "That's just what I needed to hear today. Every little thing you do matters. Every gesture has its own significance, and therein lies your excellence."

We sit quietly for a moment.

"How's Detroit these days?" I ask.

"What's beginning to unfold in Detroit is supercool," Erin responds. "Cottage industries are taking over, and I think the city is going to come back twice as strong as before. I really do. It's going to be twice as powerful, growing from a pile of small ideas. It's amazing!"

Erin's Detroit grit and pride are on full display.

"You know," Erin continues, "Detroit was a city built on just two big ideas: Motown and automobiles. When those big ideas fell, it was a bit of an abyss, because that's all there was. We were totally dependent on a few powerful people running a few powerful industries. But now, an amazing transition is taking place. Cottage industries are rising in previously abandoned buildings all across Detroit. Instead of being dependent on one or two economic giants, Detroit is rebuilding itself on thousands of smaller ideas. It's grassroots. It's organic, and really powerful, because it's diversified, and a true expression of the people. Detroit is on its way to becoming the strongest it has ever been."

The heart and soul of the new Detroit is the Seventh Power.

"When a society is at its lowest point, it's a beautiful time of opportunity," Erin continues.

Erin's words make me think of Pine Ridge and other communities in the world that have fallen victim to overreaching but haven't yet realized that the power to recover lives within them.

"My goal is to keep going, and growing. I want to open my voice more, open up to kindness more, become more approachable," Erin adds. "I'm still very competitive—I mean, I want to sell out every class—but I also want to become more open, more vulnerable. I want to let that side of me shine. Sometimes the words flow for me and sometimes they don't. I don't know why that is."

"Well, today, you are the 'girl on fire,'" I say, referencing Katniss Everdeen in *The Hunger Games*.

A few moments later we share a hug on the street corner and head our separate ways.

The world is as round or as flat as you want it to be, I think as I walk along, in no hurry at all.

* * *

A MONTH LATER I AM BACK IN BOSTON AGAIN, on my way to another SoulCycle class. Street vendors offer up lemonade and Italian ice as a small Jamaican band plays on the corner by the library. Two rows of hardwood trees border the central lawn at Copley Square, where the old and the new coexist. The John Hancock Tower, the

Fairmont Copley Plaza Hotel, Trinity Church, and SoulCycle all share the same block.

I take a deep breath.

"Ah, there's my voice," I proclaim in a momentarily healthy, normal tone. I am trying to breathe with more fluidity. I want to take more responsibility for my own voice and be less reliant on the Botox treatments. Even though I have been told my disorder is incurable, I am digging in, trying to work within myself to make it better.

I have come to Copley Square early today in order to walk inside Trinity Church.

I work my way through the scaffolding that surrounds the great church, following the signs to the entrance, where I pay seven dollars for admission. Once inside, I am enveloped by silence. Whispers echo and pews creak, but otherwise, the great hall is hushed.

Seven stained-glass windows with arches frame the circular east end of the church, behind the hanging golden symbol of the cross. Light reflects down on the white marble altar. The air is redolent with the musty smell of the slim red cushions on the pews. Each aisle has benches for kneeling, and everywhere there is carved wood and stone. Incalculable hours of craftsmanship are on display.

This old church is alive and well, but it's no longer the only place in the neighborhood to find the sacred spirit within you.

Near the front counter by the entrance, a poster reading TOP 10 REASONS FOR BEING AN EPISCOPALIAN hangs next to stacks of blue T-shirts that are for sale. My favorite: *You can believe in dinosaurs.*

Farther inside the church, along the south wall, is a passage from the Gospel according to Matthew: *They that were ready went in with him.*

For me, the passage references the personal leadership journey of making the world better by turning inward and working on ourselves. When we seek, find, and share our own true voice, we join with the sacred and the holy. SoulCycle and the Trinity Church are organizations that help people answer this call. In a flat world, everyone can, and must, lead.

* * *

TWENTY MINUTES LATER I am across the street and strapped into bike #50 as Michael Jackson's "Man in the Mirror" resounds from the speakers above.

If you wanna make the world a better place
Take a look at yourself, and then make a change

In the front of the dark studio, by the wall full of mirrors that allows everyone to bike toward their own reflection, Erin is leading class. Four candles burn at the corners of her podium beneath her elevated bike.

On the wall to her left, in bold, black letters, the following words appear:

ATHLETE
LEGEND
WARRIOR
RENEGADE
ROCK STAR
SOULCYCLE

Everything about this experience is designed to celebrate the individual spirit. This is a place where the Seventh Power is served and can thrive.

"Allow your mind to go free and search for your opportunities to grow, even if they are small," Erin says softly. Pretty soon she is going to jack the place up, but right now she is whispering, building her message—her sermon—for the day.

"Don't get comfortable—on the bike, or in life—especially if you feel like you are plateauing. That plateau is trying to tell you something."

Erin goes quiet, letting Michael Jackson and the hum of the wheels take over.

"OK, here we go," Erin says, as her voice intensifies. "Let's ride with our eyes closed and learn to trust what we can't see. Let's learn to trust what's inside. Quit hiding your magic. The world is ready for you. It's time to let your authentic self shine."

* * *

Two days later, on a business trip south, I am standing in front of my hotel on a crisp Thursday morning. My destination is Waffle House. It's my favorite breakfast experience on Earth, and you can't have it in Maine. Waffle House, for me, is a mystical encounter with breakfast excellence achieved within a concrete box of simplicity and transparency. It also happens to be one of my favorite power-dispersing business structures on Earth. So anytime I am in the American South, Waffle House, for me, is a must-do event.

"So, hon, I have a suggestion for you," Elle, my Lyft driver, says as soon as I have closed her car door. "I want to take you to a different Waffle House than the one you've selected. The one you chose is pretty old and right by the highway. It's a truck stop, really—not that I have anything against truckers; I don't. God bless them all. We need them, you know. But if you don't mind, I want to take you to this other Waffle House instead. It's just an extra mile away, and it's brand-new. I think you'll like it much better."

"That sounds fine, Elle," I say.

Our conversation goes quiet for a moment as the song "Dream Weaver" by Gary Wright plays on satellite radio. I love this classic seventies ballad from my youth. I was nine years old when it was released.

Elle sees me in her rearview mirror, checking out the song title and artist on the digital screen of the center console. "I'm a hippie through and through," Elle says with a wink and a smile.

Elle has a smile you can trust. Her hair, a peppered mix of gray and black, is pulled back into a scarf that is wrapped tightly across the top of her head.

"Once a hippie, always a hippie," I reply.

That was a time when some felt it was necessary to drop out of mainstream organizations in order to bring a deeper sense of spirituality, meaning, and self-expression into their lives. Today, leaders have the opportunity to bring self-expression and the search for meaning into the place of work as a way to make organizations more dynamic and socially valuable.

"I never really wanted to leave the seventies," Elle says, more to herself than to me. "It just ended, you know, so I kind of had to go. Part of me still lives there, I suppose. We're all just trying to find our voice," Elle continues. "It's tough out there—being yourself, I mean—knowing what you believe and understanding who you want to be."

I am always struck by statements like this. I hear them all the time now that I have awakened to the possibility that the human journey is a quest to find and release one's own true voice.

Seconds later I open the glass door to the Waffle House as a bell above me jingles, announcing my arrival. A waitress greets me before the door itself has fully closed. "Sit anywhere you like, love," she says.

Nine large white bubble lights from the same design decade as Elle's music collaborate with the morning sun to illuminate this small rectangular building of glass and brick. Familiarity is part of the allure here. A Waffle House is a Waffle House, no matter where you go. I admire both the predictability and the variability of the place. I can see the entire operation from my seat. Every waitress, cook, and customer are visible. Every cooking station is in plain sight. At Waffle House, there is nowhere to hide. This is a place where transparency dominates, the manager is hard to find, and every employee is meant to be a leader who is seen and heard. This does not mean the customer experience is always amazing, but it does mean the experience is always fully in the hands of the employees. Accountability rules at Waffle House, and that's why I love it here. Waffle House is a human breakfast adventure.

I hold up the large laminated menu as if greeting an old friend. I revel in my options for ordering hash browns. I can get them "smothered, covered, scattered, or topped." I am not totally sure what the differences are and briefly wonder if my waitress will be disappointed if I order them plain.

A lady soon arrives and stands over me. "Welcome to Waffle House, love. My name is Kelly. I'll be your waitress this morning. What can we make you for breakfast today?"

Kelly is wearing tan pants and a gray shirt beneath a black apron, on which is pinned her yellow name tag. Her hair is thick and wavy, held tight by a visor. She strikes me as a mom's mom and a grandma's grandma. In her presence I feel like an honored guest.

Kelly takes my order the old-fashioned way: with a pencil on a small handheld pad (with carbon paper, no less). She tucks the pencil behind her ear when she's done.

"My, oh my, that sounds lovely," Kelly says, shaking her head and humming as she recounts my order: "So that's scrambled eggs with cheese, wheat toast, a sausage patty, and hash browns scattered with cheese." I feel like I just made the best possible choice in the whole wide world, proud to have selected something "scattered."

Waffle House is all about transparency, which positions it well to thrive in the modern age. You select your own seat. You can sit at the counter, just a few feet away from the grill, or choose a booth anywhere you like. Once your order is placed, you can then watch it all unfold. You can see and hear the eggs break, then sizzle. You can see and hear your plate hit the counter. You can even hear your toast being buttered. There are no mysteries regarding the status of your order. The waitress sees the cook, and the cook sees the customer. It's hard to even imagine the role of the manager here. The transparency of the system governs itself.

As I wait for my breakfast to be cooked and served, I look out the window at the big yellow Waffle House sign with block letters. A sign like this can be found on pretty much every highway exit from Delaware to Florida, and then all the way across the Midwest to Texas. Most people probably drive right by these yellow concrete buildings without recognizing the social contribution Waffle House is quietly making by guiding humanity toward a flat organizational model where everyone leads. The Sioux tribes on the northern plains knew long ago that organizations function best when power is dispersed. Who would have guessed that this breakfast chain would be one of the modern keepers of this sacred wisdom?

I look around the room and smile, quite certain that no one else here is thinking what I'm thinking. "You're crazy," I whisper.

Before I know it Kelly is back with my food. She lays the oval white plate in front of me. "Boy oh boy, love, that looks good! Enjoy," she says.

When breakfast is done I slide out of the booth and head toward the exit. On my way out I hand Kelly a ten-dollar tip for a ten-dollar meal. She made my morning, and then I made hers. The world can function quite well that way. The power of princes and presidents pales in comparison to what all the world's strangers can do just by being nice to each other.

Moments later I am in the back of Eddie's black Buick Regal, my ride arranged once again through Lyft.

"What do you mean, you ain't got no Waffle Houses up north?" Eddie says with a mixture of surprise and indignation.

I shrug my shoulders and smile in response.

We drive for a mile or so before arriving at the scene of a two-car accident. The police and fire department have arrived, and everyone appears to be OK, but the cars are still in the middle of the road beneath the blinking red light that seems to say, "I told you so."

"How the hell does that happen?" Eddie asks rhetorically. "I'll tell you what, I see it every day. People don't pay no attention anymore. You got to pay attention for them. People is always on their phones or hurryin' or worryin' or doing somethin'. I don't know what people is thinkin' 'bout, but it sure ain't drivin'. People ain't payin' no attention anymore."

A few minutes later I am back where I started.

"Thanks for the ride, Eddie. It was nice talking with you," I say.

"All right, man—I appreciate that, man. I do my best, you know. You take care of yourself now."

I linger outside for a few minutes, enjoying the crisp morning.

At Lyft, power is dispersed. The taxi industry has evolved as well, but it still brings forth the bureaucratic image of central dispatch. I picture an old warehouse on the edge of town where the yellow, uncomfortable cars pour out into the city. Deep inside a roughly constructed office sits the dispatcher, the taxi equivalent of the Wizard of Oz, sending forth commands so the cars know where to go.

It all makes me reflect back upon Maddy, Erin, and the yellow bikes that go nowhere.

SoulCycle is a company that gains its corporate power by helping its customers authentically self-actualize, one rider at a time. This is first achieved by giving the freedom of self-expression and individuation to its instructors. I have come to believe that if a company sets its employees free, the customer will be thrilled in return. SoulCycle is on a roll, and that is a reflection of its commitment to releasing the Seventh Power that dwells within us all.

Learning to make the headquarters smaller is a strategy that's manifesting in many places, both new and old. At Waffle House there are the customer, the waitress, and the cook in a yellow concrete box without interior walls. At Lyft, all you see are the driver and the rider, and they each share the power in contracting for a ride. At SoulCycle, the instructor's authentic self-expression gives permission and courage for riders to do the same.

In all cases, the individual, not the corporate center, is the focus of attention. The goal is to make the ego of the capital smaller. It's not all about "the company" or "the state." Like the stage I stood on at the NSDA conference, both are simply platforms for a higher calling. The planet is for individuals. Those individuals come together for a variety of important reasons, but ultimately, all life is singular and personal. Humanity evolves one soul at a time. The company is a social construct, but its people are real.

Learning to shrink the center, serve the individual human spirit, and localize a business is the fourth lesson of the age of shared leadership.

CHAPTER 5

Seeds of Peace

"The more we can be in a relationship with those who might seem strange to us, the more we can feel like we're neighbors and all members of the human family."

—MISTER ROGERS

Federal prosecutor Nick Lewin has had quite a morning. Around 9:00, he left the rustic summer camp on Pleasant Lake and turned right, walking up Mayberry Hill Road to the start of the Casco Days road race. He strolled for ten minutes on winding pavement surrounded by pine trees, occasionally feigning something that might be construed as a stretch before arriving at a small collection of New England–style farmhouses. Shortly thereafter he reached the intersection by the dirt road where the yellow school buses were dropping runners off.

At 9:30 a.m. eleven-year-old Evan Duprey stood beneath a sea of older, taller runners as his father, Matt, fired the race gun from the back of a pickup truck somewhere up ahead. At that moment six hundred race participants cheered then lunged forward. First you walked, then you jogged, then you ran. Space opened and then closed until each competitor found their early stride.

Evan broke through each small opening in the pack that he could find, setting his mental sights on Casco Village and the finish line, four miles away. Nick was more patient. This was a fun run, and the idea of actually winning never entered his mind. Evan and Nick would not meet that day despite crossing paths several times during the race, and later, on the fairgrounds in Casco Days Park.

Near the finish line, Evan's grandparents Bob and Anita waited. Bob himself was an accomplished marathoner, having amassed more than thirty thousand miles in his career, and looking like he could easily run more.

Just a few yards away, Nick's wife, Leslie, and their six-year-old daughter, Molly, waited together behind the red lemonade stand as the runners made their last big push. Leslie wore tan pants and a green T-shirt with a white logo that read SEEDS OF PEACE. Molly, wearing sandals, shorts, and a T-shirt, looked through the gaps in the crowd for her dad to summit the last hill and turn left for the finish line. Leslie and Molly would never meet Bob and Anita that day, yet their paths would also cross multiple times.

We often don't know the full story of the amazing person we just walked by.

* * *

TWENTY-NINE MINUTES AND THIRTY-FOUR SECONDS after the race begins, Evan finishes, sprinting hard, completing the race one second behind the fastest time for his age. "*One second*," Evan would later think to himself, proud of the race he'd run, yet wishing he could claw back time and find two seconds.

Five minutes and thirty seconds later, Nick crosses the line. Nearby, my wife, Alison, watches it all unfold. As the volunteer race coordinator, she is both pleased and relieved to see yet another successful event drift toward its natural conclusion.

This is the eighty-third annual Casco Days celebration, a revered tradition in this small lakeside town.

Thirty minutes after completing the race and still wearing his running gear, Nick is once again hard at work. This time he finds himself under a small red-and-white carnival tent with Molly. Both wear Hancock Lumber carpenter's nailing aprons while children hurl dimes toward them (and sometimes at them) from three sides. Neither Nick nor Molly has time to look up. They are both watching for winning throws and sweeping away the unsuccessful coins with their bare hands into the white collection tray that surrounds the game board.

On the board itself are two dozen images of a black-and-white panda sitting upright and smiling. The object of the game is to toss your dime with just the right combination of spin, altitude, and luck so as to land it completely inside one of the furry mammal outlines.

"Oh, look there—I won! I won!" a young child exclaims, pointing anxiously at his dime that has come to rest in the middle of one happy panda's belly. The boy is jumping up and down and tugging at his mother's arm. His mother, already holding five other stuffed animals, pretends to share his excitement.

As Nick sweeps a small mountain of dimes off the board, Molly hands the enthusiastic winner a soft, stuffed toy candle modeled loosely after the lovable character Lumière in Disney's animated classic Beauty and the Beast.

"If you win one more time, you can trade that in for the big one," Molly says, luring him back for more as she points to the even larger animated candles hanging from the chicken wire on the back of the tent.

In nearby tents coins are also being tossed as stuffed tigers, dolphins, teddy bears, elephants, and giant multicolored lizards all wait to see who will take them home. The music plays as the merry-go-round turns. High above, children throw their hands in the air as the Ferris wheel rises, then descends. Steam pours from the vent above the food booth as hamburgers, hot dogs, and sausages sizzle.

On this day you would have no idea that Nick Lewin makes a living prosecuting terrorists for the United States Attorney's Office in Manhattan. Nor would you know that his wife, Leslie, is the executive director of perhaps the most effective and dynamic youth peace camp in the entire world. Nick chases terrorists, and Leslie works generationally to mitigate the conditions that create them. That's big stuff on both ends.

But today is Casco Days.... Tomorrow the Lewins can go back to saving the world.

* * *

IT'S TUESDAY, THREE DAYS LATER. It's a classic Maine summer day with blue sky, low humidity, and a gentle breeze. As I drive down the Mayberry Hill Road, I pass the starting line for the Casco Days road race before turning left into the Seeds of Peace Camp. A Maine state trooper emerges with a clipboard from the small white guardhouse and checks me in before opening the blue-and-green gate by hand.

Flags ring the entrance to the grounds, signaling that something of global significance happens here. The emblems on display include the town of Otisfield, Maine, the United Nations, Israel,

Palestine, Egypt, Jordan, India, Pakistan, Afghanistan, the United Kingdom, Canada, Greece, Turkey, Morocco, Tunisia, Qatar, Yemen, Bosnia, Macedonia, and Cyprus. This camp has taken on the pursuit of peace through engaging teenagers in some of the toughest conflict zones on Earth, and the circle of flags stands as testimony to this mission.

I didn't even know Otisfield had a flag, I think jealously and momentarily distracted, having lived in neighboring flagless Casco all my life.

I park just a short distance away under a row of towering pine trees facing the lake. Nearby, campers are swimming, splashing, and diving. The phrase "The way life could be" is painted in green on a white picket fence. The setting is serene, highly conducive to the mission of this global peace camp, tucked away on the northeast corner of a little-known lake in an even lesser-known town.

My host, Dick Romeo, walks up the dirt path toward me. A Seeds of Peace veteran, Dick is helping to facilitate the camp's final program of the summer.

The first session of camp, featuring Israeli, Palestinian, Egyptian, and Jordanian teenagers, as well as campers from India and Pakistan, had ended just a few days before. Now a new set of teenagers is having their turn. This is the "United States" program, which connects American teens across political, social, and economic divides. Like their counterparts from the Middle East, these campers, with their diverse backgrounds, arrive with some hardwired perspectives.

Dick greets me with a warm smile and a gentle handshake that communicates mindfulness and trust. Dick has white hair and wears a green, short-sleeved Seeds of Peace shirt with a handmade name tag on his chest. His shorts are tan, and his sneakers are New Balance, possibly made right here in Maine.

"All the kids who come here have about half the story right," Dick says as he motions for me to join him for a walking tour of the lakeside campus. "But that's what brings them here. They realize this is an opportunity to expand their own self-awareness. Even though they all volunteer to come here, the dialogue process we use at camp blows them away at first. It gets confusing in a hurry, as they quickly find themselves revisiting their own tribal perspectives: 'What part of my own story is real?' These kids have never really been challenged to examine their own narratives this closely. Frankly, it rocks their world. They all come with these deeply set assumptions about what's right and what's wrong, but they leave realizing there is a lot of gray in the world—more than they previously thought."

Dick pauses and then continues. "This camp program is about having the courage to engage. We don't bring the students here to change their minds. We bring them here to give them the ability to hear stuff they strongly disagree with. That's more powerful."

This pedagogy reminds me of our own communication aspirations at Hancock Lumber. The only mind we each need to open is our own. Conformity of thought is an outdated goal, from a receding era of centralized power. The magic of a free society is that no two humans see the entire scene the same way. Listen for understanding, not judgment. It's respect for the diversity of thought that creates unity.

The crunching noise of footsteps on the path reminds me of the dry ground of the Pine Ridge Indian Reservation.

For the longest time I struggled to explain to people what I did with my time at Pine Ridge. The truth was, I didn't really do anything when I was there. Each day I traveled around and sat with my friends. We just visited. Only rarely did we discuss strategies for social transformation. I didn't feel any desire to create change at Pine Ridge. The people of Pine Ridge were all amazing to me as they were. They were fully capable of creating their own future.

In time I came to realize that being present was, in itself, a pathway to change. Awareness and connectivity are power acts. For generations (white) people from away have traveled to Pine Ridge to fix, save, and change the people who live there. But that has not worked, because sustainable change only comes from within.

I traveled to Pine Ridge without any formal role. My only responsibility was as a human. Once there I met people and hung out with them. I was interested in their story, culture, and traditions. But I also saw the larger relationship. The Oglala are a subset of the Lakota. The Lakota are a subset of the Sioux. The Sioux are a subset of the varied Native American tribes. The Native American tribes are a subset of the planet's indigenous communities. The planet's indigenous communities are a subset of the human race. We all come from different tribes, *and* we all come from the same tribe. It just depends on the frame of reference one chooses.

It's similar for me at work. When I travel around our company, I don't see employees. I see people who have jobs. The frame of reference matters. We see what we want to see.

Are we different? Yes.

Are we the same? Yes.

Transcending the urge to judge, fix, solve, or transform others is what actually creates the conditions for communities (or companies) to progress. When people feel heard, not judged, they relax. When people relax, they think. When people think, they grow.

As Hellen Keller once said, "Although the world is full of suffering, it is also full of the overcoming of it."

"The first step is to help each camper learn how to look inward, to look hardest at themselves and get more deeply connected to who they are as a person," Dick says. "Only then are they ready to engage effectively with others."

This statement reminds me of SoulCycle and its focus on advancing the human spirit, one soul at a time. Humanity only changes when individuals change. Individuals only change from within.

"It's encouraging, like seeing with fresh eyes, when you remove blame and winning from the equation," I say. "And it's transformational when you realize that *you* are the one who has to change instead of the 'other guy' across the way."

The dirt path we are on meanders away from the lake between rows of seasonal cabins with names like "Loon," "Deer," "Moose," and "Bear."

"This is where the campers come every day to sit, reflect, listen, and share ideas," Dick says. "It's where the dialogue sessions take place, where the heavy lifting occurs. Here we invite each camper to get 'into the river.'"

"*Into the river*," I echo. "I love that phrase. What does it mean here?"

"The teenagers who attend this camp come from areas of social tension and conflict. As a result, their communities often have entrenched, even dangerous, dynamics," Dick replies. "If we liken conflict to a river, we can imagine that the conflicting groups within a society live on opposing banks. The teens that come to camp are used to hurling stones across the river at their perceived enemy. As a result, they arrive prepared to show the other side that they are wrong. But at Seeds of Peace, we mix it all up on them. We invite everyone to just come into the river and swim together. We invite them into the water not to win a debate or change anyone's mind. In fact, we encourage them to stop judging and debating altogether. We just invite them to get in there and swim. To enter dialogue with an open mind is what we call 'getting into the river.'"

This causes me to reflect on the historic divide between managers and workers and how "*getting into the river*" could create value for companies. Anywhere there is a divide, there is a river.

We pause to look around and then resume our walk.

"Personal change begins day one at camp," Dick says. "Looking inward at our own assumptions is the foundation for everything else that happens here."

All around us teenagers come and go from their rustic cabins. Screen doors spring open before bouncing to a close. Transparency is a theme here, and the cabins themselves are symbolic of this value, with their mesh screens that allow views of each building and beyond, to the lake behind. There is nowhere to hide here.

"In summary, our program has three core components," Dick explains. "First and foremost, there is personal change. Without this critical ingredient, no further progress is possible."

The Lakota were keepers of this same wisdom long ago as they followed the seasons and the buffalo. The vision-quest rite encouraged each member of the tribe to find his own sense of truth. You left your village to find your voice. You returned to share it and live it authentically. The power of the tribe was derived from the power of the individual. If each person was whole, balanced, and true to his or her own voice, then the tribe would be strong. Truth was personal, and you had to seek it.

This indigenous wisdom is being given new life right here on the banks of Pleasant Lake. The campers, on the verge of entering adulthood, leave their communities and journey out alone into a strange new land. Here they are met by a diverse collection of people and perspectives. Here they are encouraged to sit, listen, and look inward. It's a modern-day vision quest in a Seeds of Peace T-shirt.

"Once we have established the groundwork for personal change, a whole new world materializes," Dick continues. "Personal change is the pathway to interpersonal change. This is the second phase of our program. Once we have asked each camper to see themselves differently, we then invite them to engage with a single person differently. Often, that person is someone who comes from a very different place than you do, perhaps even someone you grew up seeing as your enemy, the one who caused your problems. So only after working on interpersonal change do we enter a zone where larger societal transformation becomes possible."

The pedagogy of this camp is refreshing and aligned with so much of what I have learned from my voice condition and subsequent time at Pine Ridge. We must create change first and foremost within ourselves. Only then are we ready to embrace another human and be present in a way that supports their own change.

In hindsight, I can see my own management career in two distinct buckets: there is me before SD, and there is me after SD. The twenty years of managing before SD were externally focused. I was absorbed in a traditional management approach, focused on how other people needed change. When they didn't change to my satisfaction, I got dogmatic. When people didn't come around, I just intensified my speeches.

Of course, that didn't create change. People just stopped overtly resisting. I pushed the diversity of thought essential to a healthy company underground. Excellence, from this approach, was impossible.

But then I lost a piece of my voice, and pushing my way through the world verbally was no longer possible. I had to say less and listen more. In time this helped me see a new path. The partial loss of my own voice was an invitation to strengthen the voices of others. This is what brought me to the notion of dispersed power and shared leadership. It was only then that our company took off and my life got easier.

When people feel judged, their willingness to consider alternative perspectives narrows. Conversely, when people feel respected, they become more open to expanding their views. This is one of the biggest learning opportunities for managers and supervisors in the age of shared leadership. It's not necessary to refute or redirect views that differ from your own. The purpose of listening is not judgment. The objective of listening is understanding.

"One person at a time adds up," Dick says, referring to nearly seven thousand Seeds of Peace alumni from twenty-seven countries.

We've come to a small, three-sided, lean-to structure whose walls carry the seal of the United Nations and an inscription from the former secretary-general Kofi Annan:

There can be no more important initiative than bringing together young people who have seen the ravages of war to learn the art of peace.

Seeds of Peace is certainly an example of the world the United Nations is actively working for.

"This is where we'll be working with the students today," Dick says, gesturing toward a single-story cabin nearby. "This is the Trophy Room, where the old Camp Powhatan [the camp that operated on this site before Seeds of Peace] plaques, recognizing the sporting-event champions from each season of camp, still line the walls."

The old building is nestled into a grove of large pine trees. Moss has accumulated on the green shingled roof, and the front porch is lined with white benches. Behind the benches, a row of white wooden windows is swung open. Inside, a large stone fireplace occupies the opposite wall.

Dick removes his shoes on the porch and walks inside, and I do the same. Moments later the campers begin to arrive.

Dick invited me here today for some dialogue with a small group of returning second-year campers known as the Paradigm Shifters. The majority of the Seeds who come here attend only once, but a few are invited to return for a second year, to delve even deeper into their own personal development, and to serve as peer mentors for the rest of the camp community.

In small groups, the Paradigm Shifters descend upon the Trophy Room. Twenty-six, mostly rising high school seniors. About half of them are from Maine; the others are from New York City, Syracuse, Chicago, and Los Angeles. They are a diverse group.

I glance at the roster, whispering each name as the squad morphs into a cozy circle: Abdul, Aidan, Alistair, Anna, Bupalo, Davion, Fayhiyo, Izzy, Jonah, Jules, Kate, Kejuan, Kelly, Mathison, Mia, Mohamed (two of them), Molly, Najma, Nathan, Richard, Ryan, Sandhya, Sophia, Talia, and Tema. One by one they pick their spots, some sitting in plastic chairs or wooden benches, others simply plunking down cross-legged on the floor. Seeds self-organize.

Four lit candles have been placed in the middle of the circle, on the floor.

"Today we are going to visit with a local business executive who has been on an unusual journey," Dick says, launching the session as he stands before an easel. "It involves Hancock Lumber, the Pine Ridge Indian Reservation, and a voice disorder called spasmodic dysphonia. I think you will find his story timely and relevant to our mission," Dick says, taking a seat on the bench beside me.

"Thank you for having me here," I say. "Your circle is powerful. I feel honored to be in it." I share my story of how a rare voice disorder and a remote Indian reservation combined to help me see leadership as an opportunity to strengthen the voices of others.

"Good leaders make themselves smaller," I say, "so that there's room for everybody to lead and be heard. Traditionally, those who come into power overreach—they go too far. Pine Ridge is an example of what can happen when those with the most power take too much.

"It's a tale of two cultures," I say. "When the Lakota were self-directed, they were self-sufficient. Today, Pine Ridge is one of the poorest places in America. But what really changed? It was the same tribe, before and after. The culture is what changed. The tribe, long self-ruled, was now being governed from a capital with a different culture, thousands of miles away. That capital made its presence too big and the spirit of the individual too small."

As I scan the room there seems to be a lot of agreement among the independent minds.

"What you are doing here is inspiring," I say. "You are transcending tribal dogma—the stories we tell, or don't tell, to justify our view of the world. Pine Ridge helped me see my own dogma and how it was impairing my full vision. For example, even though I once taught American history, I needed to travel to Pine Ridge to realize that what I had learned in kindergarten was not actually true. Columbus had not discovered a new world. People already lived here."

I pause for a moment as the sound of finger snapping fills the room. This form of understanding and respect—the same one used in the 1950s during Beatnik poetry readings in Greenwich Village—is afforded here at camp to others when they speak with their own true voice.

"I have now been to Pine Ridge many times," I continue. "I don't have any official title or formal role when I visit; I just wander around and talk with the people who live there. It's all quite liberating, actually, to have no specific mission other than to just be connected."

It's clear the Paradigm Shifters understand the idea of connectivity without judgment.

"My time at Pine Ridge has led me to wonder if people sometimes look in the wrong places to rebuild that which has been broken. Over the course of several generations, the people of Pine Ridge were oriented to look toward Washington, DC, for solutions. Despite all efforts to make amends, I don't think the government can ever restore what it took away. This is a hard realization. Those who overreached can't, on their own, make things whole again. The circle only becomes whole when a critical mass of people transcends their grievances and remembers that sovereignty is something that lives within us all."

I stop to catch my breath. My voice is strained and tight, but sharing these ideas is important to me right now. After quickly regrouping, I reach down to my backpack and pull out a colorful necklace.

"This is a Lakota medicine wheel," I say, pointing to the pendant at the bottom. "It represents the Six Great Powers, or Grandfathers, of Lakota spirituality. The West, North, East, South, Sky, and Earth are all honored here. But some at Pine Ridge who know the old ways say that a Seventh Power also exists, right here at the very center of the wheel itself. The Seventh Power is you. The Seventh Power is me. It's the difference a single, engaged, and self-aware individual can make in the world.

"It is symbolic that the Seventh Power lives at the very center of the sacred wheel. Wherever you go, you stand at the center of your world. When you move, the center moves too. When you think about it, unlocking the Seventh Power is the Seeds of Peace leadership model. First, you work on yourself. Only then can you sit peacefully with another. Entire societies can be transformed with this knowledge. Change is created locally. We learn first to make peace within ourselves so that we can then be present for others, without judgment. You and your circle are tapping back into an important piece of indigenous wisdom and giving it new life in the modern age.

"Now," I say, "I would like to hear your stories. Tell me, what brings you here? Or should I say, what brings you back here for a second experience?"

Abdul, to my left, speaks first. "Well, really, I came back here because Seeds of Peace helps me learn how to be the best possible version of myself." Abdul has dark spiked hair and wide, inquisitive eyes. He is wearing a gray hooded sweatshirt underneath a green Seeds of Peace T-shirt.

"This camp has given me a safe place to step outside my comfort zone. Once that happened I began to see that I was quite different than I thought I was. It was like a new person was born inside me. I guess I needed to get outside my own community to really begin to learn more about who I was—to learn more about my own voice," Abdul says, and then pauses. "It's safe here," he continues. "That's what I like most. It's a safe place to practice being me and to learn to engage with others differently. I can practice being me here and then bring it back home."

More finger snaps of solidarity fill the Trophy Room.

Next, Aidan jumps in from his seat on the floor. "I came back to Seeds of Peace because this sort of community doesn't really exist outside this place. People just support you here; they let you be who you are, and don't judge what you think or say.

"It's more difficult back home to foster trust with people," Aidan continues. "But trust is a priority here. This is not a competitive environment. There is space for conflict here, but the word *conflict* takes on a whole new meaning. I mean, people have different perspectives here too, but it's not combative in any way. It's respectful. Seeds of Peace allows me to work on who I am, which makes me, in turn, more accepting of others. When my own confidence grows, I feel more able to connect with other people. Seeds has strengthened how I feel about myself."

Najma is from Portland, Maine, by way of Minneapolis, by way of Africa. "Umm…to be honest, I debated over whether I wanted to come back or not this year," Najma says as she looks down and adjusts her position on the floor. "I was torn, because I didn't want to be disappointed. I didn't want to risk the pain of being vulnerable. Opening up and sharing our most private experiences can be difficult. I don't know anyone who likes to be vulnerable."

Najma pauses. The room waits.

"In the end, I came back because I believe in the vision here, and I did want to challenge myself to keep growing. It's painful sometimes to look inside ourselves, to confront our past, but I think maybe it's not as difficult in the long run as avoiding it."

People nod their heads and snap their fingers some more. The conversation has an easy flow to it. Each camper in the circle seems to know just the right moment to add another perspective.

Kejuan, also sitting on the floor, is the next to share.

"For me it was pretty difficult leaving camp the first time. I remember riding home on the train from O'Hare to the South Side of Chicago, where I live. It's not the best area. I was sitting on the train looking out at the graffiti, and…it all looked different to me. I was confused. It was like I was moving back and forth between two completely different worlds."

Kejuan stops briefly and adjusts one of his socks. Even though he is big and strong, he speaks with a soft, vulnerable tone. "There's this stop on the train where all the white people get off. Then the train keeps going to where I live. It was really difficult coming back home after camp the first time. There were something like one hundred shootings on the South Side alone in just the two weeks I was gone.

"It was a pretty big struggle for me after camp," Kejuan says. "My family moved a lot. I went to three different schools my sophomore year. All the while I just kept wondering how my life would be different if I was always at Seeds of Peace—if I could just stay here. In my world in Chicago, you can't just say hi to someone when you walk past them. I wanted to reach out to people, but it's just not a place where you can do that. You have to be careful all the time about who you talk to and what you say. I lost some friends after camp. I couldn't really talk to all of them the same way anymore, and I think it threw them off. It was hard. My perspectives had changed. I was seeing the world differently, but it was complicated to know how to share these new perspectives back home. It got confusing. My guard went down as soon as I got off the bus back here. I knew I was somewhere safe again."

I let out a deep, slow breath, thinking about how brave Kejuan is.

Kate from Pasadena is sitting in a white plastic chair to Kejuan's left. She has long, curly blonde hair, and is the next to contribute.

"In my community, my school is very competitive. A lot of people think mostly about themselves—their grades, their future," Kate says. "This camp is the most diverse community I have ever been a part of, and it feels really good to connect more broadly. That's what brought me back here, I think: connecting with a broader, more diverse community."

Finger snaps of approval and support reverberate around the room.

"The method of healing here is special," Kate says. "We really get to the core here. We talk about the real issues. Back home all the conversations are more surface-level stuff. Here it's deep, and it's real. It makes a difference."

The word *healing* resonates for me. We are all taught to hold it together on the outside, but the truth is, everyone acquires wounds, and therefore, everyone needs to heal. Healing is necessary in order to ascend the ladder of consciousness.

"Healing requires being honest with yourself," Kate says. "All of us in this room, we are the same, and yet different, and that forces us to really figure out who we are as individuals. This camp has helped me take a deep look at who I am. Getting to know myself better makes me feel more whole."

We are all "in the river" now, and everyone takes a turn. Each Seed shares and each Seed listens. Nothing is solved or accomplished in a practical sense, yet something extraordinary unfolds in this small cabin. It's the opportunity for authentic, safe dialogue.

One could truly change the whole world this way, one teenager at a time.

* * *

A FEW DAYS LATER I AM SITTING in the Hancock Lumber conference room on the opposite corner of the lake from the Seeds of Peace Camp. The high ceiling is covered in lightly stained pine boards made at our Casco sawmill, just a few miles away. On the end wall is a large buffalo head mount from a recent hunting trip in Wyoming, on former Lakota tribal lands, from which I took the meat to the reservation and shared it with the community there.

To my left, Leslie Lewin, executive director of Seeds of Peace, is sitting in front of the large TV monitor beneath the Best Places to Work in Maine banner. This banner makes me happy every time I look at it, because I know how hard it is to earn one.

Leslie knows a lot about highly engaged teams, and I am pleased to be sharing time with her. With her long, dark hair and fair skin, Leslie looks like everyone's best friend. Beneath her down-to-earth aura, however, there is a well-trained and extremely talented leader, who is all about dispersing power.

Leslie graduated from the University of Pennsylvania and earned a master's degree from NYU's Wagner Graduate School of Public Service. Her dad, a former camper at Camp Powhatan, was so struck by his camp experience in Maine that he returned time and time again to Pleasant Lake as an adult with his own family.

Twenty years ago Leslie was hired to teach tennis at the Seeds of Peace Camp, and today she leads the entire organization. A Boston girl living in Brooklyn, she still loves the Red Sox, and a small lake in Maine has become her second home.

"Pleasant Lake keeps my sanity," Leslie says with a smile, leaning back comfortably in her chair.

"Tell me more about the camp," I say.

"Think about it," Leslie says, shifting slightly forward. "Pakistanis meet Indians here for the first time; Israeli Jews engage Palestinian Muslims; kids from Chicago's South Side meet kids from suburban Portland, Maine. It all happens right here in Otisfield, Maine, of all places. They're not only meeting for the first time, but also sitting, eating, and sleeping side by side, in dialogue. It's pretty transformational. Our program is really about creating the skills and the space for intaking the identities and stories of others. It's an identity-seeking experience. First, you stop and contemplate your own identity. This enables you to then take in the identities of others. We are creating spaces and configurations that just don't really happen otherwise."

"It's all about engagement, isn't it?" I ask. "It's all about being willing to get uncomfortable and engage your own carefully selected view of the world in a different way."

"Yes," Leslie replies. "We tell the Seeds on the opening night of camp that it would be easier not to hear these stories, the stories of people and communities that you may have long perceived to be the enemy. In a lot of ways it's safer to just stay home and continue to see the world in black and white. But at Seeds of Peace Camp, we teach people to see the gray. We need to learn to see the gray, to get comfortable with it. The world is a much richer place when it's gray."

We smile at each other.

"We all need to get uncomfortable," Leslie says. "That discomfort is where the growth and opportunities live. We need to hear the other side of the story—the half we are missing."

"I love the idea of learning to intake the identities and stories of others," I say. "Connectivity and awareness without judgment are powerful acts."

* * *

TWO DAYS LATER I AM BACK in the Trophy Room to meet with Dick and six Paradigm Shifters from across America. Every window is cranked open to let the cool summer air drift through the screens. Like the STAR School on the edge of the Navajo reservation, nature permeates here.

Najma, Kejuan, Izzy, Kate, Abdul, and Aidan have each volunteered to come back to talk with me.

"What is the biggest challenge your community faces back home?" I ask.

Najma is the first to speak. "Trauma. My community is made up of African refugees. We are dealing with lots of internalized trauma from war and violence." Najma pauses, then continues. "I see it a lot—all around me, in fact—first-generation refugee kids. Their parents suffered from such extreme trauma that it has almost been passed down, almost hereditary, as crazy as that sounds. Our community also suffers from a lot of mental illness, drug abuse, tribalism, and self-hate, while the larger society pretends not to know why."

My dear friend and Dakota elder, Catherine Grey Day, said something similar to me when we first met.

"It's internalized," Catherine said. "Our oppression as a people is internalized."

"What do you mean by that, Catherine?" I asked.

"It's just about being worn down, generation after generation. The cavalry, the missionaries, the government, the boarding schools—you wake up one day and it has all been internalized. When you have been oppressed over generations and generations, it finally takes hold. The oppression takes hold within you. Once it takes hold within you, it is perpetuated from within, and we act out the oppression on ourselves. That is how deeply it has been ingrained."

A silence came over us.

"Change comes from within," Catherine said, breaking the reflective pause. "Our progress as a people must come from within."

Najma has never met Catherine Grey Day. In fact, they were born in different eras, yet both understand the same cycle of overreaching, despair, and recovery. Najma calls it "internalized trauma"; Catherine calls it "internalized oppression." The root causes and outcomes are the same. In both cases, those who held power overreached. Those who lost power have yet to feel secure and safe enough to look inward, to the sacred place where you get it back. It's a cycle as old as humanity itself.

"Violence," Kejuan chimes in. "That's Chicago's challenge. There are lots of shootings and stuff right in my neighborhood. As a result, when I am home, I stay inside most of the time. We go downtown to hang out because it is safer there. But going downtown is hard in a different way. The way they stop us for no reason, the police and store security guards—it makes me angry. Like, if I go into a store on Michigan Avenue to buy something, I hold my money in my hand on purpose so the guard can see I am going to buy it, not steal it. And then I go back home, and there are guys in cars with guns in their laps. It's crazy."

I attempt to imagine what that feels like.

Izzy, like Najma, is from Portland, and says, "Ignorance is the biggest challenge in my community—people just being too comfortable in their own bubbles and not really having any interest or awareness on a broader level. I have been exposed to so much diversity here at camp—so many amazing people, so many difficult stories that are not present in my community—but I needed to hear them. The world is bigger than our own little bubbles. Complacency, because it's not a problem in my bubble, is the biggest challenge I see back home."

I thank everyone for their courage and authenticity. We all hug, and then the Seeds leave.

"You have to take care of the box you live in first, before you can go out of that square constructively," Dick says to me as we stand outside under the towering pines. "Tim Wilson, our former camp director, would always say that at the opening-night gathering of camp."

"That's such an empowering perspective," I reply. "It puts both the opportunity and responsibility for change squarely in your hands."

Dick and I shake hands and part ways.

In the days that followed my conversations with the Paradigm Shifters, I found myself wondering about the origins of this progressive yet simple pedagogy of leadership. These teenagers were spending just two or three weeks at camp and leaving with a skill set capable of altering the future of an entire planet, filled with billions of humans. How did that come about? Who made that happen? Who broke the code of complexity?

* * *

AT YORDPROM COFFEE CO., on the uphill side of Congress Street just a few blocks from the Maine Medical Center campus in Portland, I meet Tim Wilson. It is 9:00 a.m. on the last day of summer, and you can feel autumn in the air. Tim is the founding camp director at Seeds of Peace and still deeply engaged, although retired from a formal role.

I am using both hands to hold a large red cup filled with hot chocolate. In the center a little bit of whipped cream swirls like a slow-motion view of a hurricane from above. To my left, past the open screen door, other customers sip their coffees, read their papers, and chat at the blue metal tables and chairs on the patio.

"They leave with a toolbox," Tim says of the kids who graduate from the Seeds of Peace program each summer. Tim is leaning back in his chair, wearing a black sweat suit with gray accents over a white T-shirt. His legs are stretched out in front of him. He wears a black Tuskegee Airmen hat. "Their job is to then go back home and engage the various entities at their school and share what they've learned. They can often be change agents because they have some skills that other kids might not have."

"How did all of this come about, Tim?" I ask. "What brought you to Seeds of Peace?"

Tim pulls off his hat with one hand and passes the other through his short gray hair. "It was 1960 at Slippery Rock University," Tim says. "I was at spring football practice, and this guy Joel Bloom showed up. He was a friend of one of my coaches. The next thing you know, Coach called me over and asked me if I would like to be a counselor at Mr. Bloom's camp in Maine.

"I said, 'Let me get this straight, Mr. Bloom,'" Tim says. "'You want a Negro from Pittsburgh to come to Maine for the summer and work as a counselor at an all-Jewish boys' camp?'" Tim pauses and chuckles. "Sure enough, that summer, off I went.

"So I was a counselor at Camp Powhatan from 1960 to 1962. Then I spent three years in the Peace Corps before returning to camp in 1966. In 1968 I became head counselor, and in 1970 they made me assistant camp director. This place has been a big part of my life ever since.

"Maine just came into my life," Tim says. "Let me tell you something: there weren't a lot of black dudes in Maine back then," he says, raising his eyebrows for emphasis. "I remember going up to Dexter High School in the summer of 1966 to interview to be their head football and wrestling coach. I told them beforehand over the telephone that I was black, just to make sure there were no surprises or misunderstandings when I got there."

Over time, Tim Wilson paved new ground here in Maine. After Dexter, he coached at the University of Maine and later held cabinet positions for governors Kenneth Curtis, a Democrat, and James B. Longley, an Independent, in the state capital, Augusta.

"I was the first 'energy czar' in America," Tim says, still smiling. "I remember sitting down there in the basement of the Cross Office Building, in my suit and tie, trying to figure out what the hell I was going to do next. I mean, what did I know about energy?"

"What's the source of it all, though, Tim?" I ask. "Where did the skills and leadership development systems you've helped create at Seeds of Peace come from? How did you figure out that formula?"

Tim considers the question before responding. There is no hurry here this morning.

"There's a bunch of people who raised me," Tim replies. "Coaches, teachers, neighbors, guidance counselors, and so forth, but I've got to say, it was my parents who taught me the core skills I use today. That's where it all started—with my parents." Tim chuckles. "It was my dad who taught me that I have two ears and one mouth for a reason.

"My parents moved from South Carolina to Pittsburgh in 1921. My dad took a job at U.S. Steel. I believe he was about the first black man they ever hired. He was the janitor there for forty-three years and became a bit of a legend at U.S. Steel before he was done."

Tim pauses.

"My dad, his name was Henry, he had a sixth-grade education, but I never met a man who was brighter," Tim continues. "Everyone loved and respected my dad. He was the one who taught me how to work and live in the society I was going to be faced with. You see, we grew up in Bellevue, Pennsylvania, and from the first grade until my sophomore year, I was the only black person in my entire school.

"Our neighborhood was so mixed up racially," Tim continues. "That's where it started for me, learning about how to get along across cultures. I had four best friends on the block we grew up on. One was German, one was Italian, one was Scotch-Irish, and the other was Chinese. He was the best athlete of us all, actually, but his parents wouldn't let him play school sports. He had to work at the family store.

"My mom was just as sharp as my dad," Tim says. "Mamie Mobley Wilson was the cleaning lady at Suburban General Hospital, just around the corner from where we lived. She was the cleaning lady, all right, but before she was done she practically ran the place. Everybody loved her too."

I feel as if I can see Tim's extraordinary ordinary parents strolling by in their old neighborhood.

"I went to Jackson Elementary and then Grant Middle School. Everything was named after the Civil War back then," Tim says, laughing once again.

"I was not a nice person when I was young," Tim says, looking right at me. "I had a lot to learn. I had a bad temper. I needed guidance. I needed mentoring and coaching. I punched this guy who had been elbowing me all practice, so Coach kicked me out. I didn't care, really. I didn't like basketball that much anyway."

Tim pauses.

"The same was true for football, actually. I mean, I loved football, but I didn't finish a game my freshman or sophomore year. The other teams always knew how to get me going. Someone would call me 'nigger,' and off I'd go, fighting, and the next thing you know, I was out of the game. Finally, my coach, Bruce Adams, came over to my house, and we all had a real sit-down. After Coach left, my dad said, 'Tim, if you ever get responding like that again just because someone throws the word *nigger* at you, you and I are going down to the basement.' Now, my dad was a gentle, loving man, but when he said something like that, you knew not to test him."

Tim sits up in his seat. I look down and see that my hot cocoa is nearly gone.

"That's how I was taught—that there needed to be a different way. I needed a different set of tools if I was going to make an impact in this world," Tim says. "I realized I couldn't just go around fighting everybody and being mad at the world all the time.

"Seeds of Peace held its first session during the last two weeks of August 1993," Tim continues. "The camp was founded through the vision of John Wallach. He was the longtime foreign editor for Hearst Newspapers. He had spent considerable time covering the Middle East, and while he came to believe that things could be different, he knew a fresh approach was going to be required. He had this idea for a camp and set out to find one in Maine. That quest brought him to Camp Powhatan. That's how we met and became connected. It's pretty crazy, actually, the coincidence of it all. By 1997, the summer camp economy in Maine had evolved, and Camp Powhatan closed. Seeds of Peace took over."

Tim ended up running the Seeds of Peace summer program until 2006 and has stayed closely connected since. Today, he is a bit of an ambassador at large, coming and going from camp during the summer and representing the Maine program in the state during the off-season. The program is Tim's baby, and he will likely look out for it as long as he walks this Earth.

"The biggest reason we have been so successful is because of our approach to dialogue. Back in Portland, during the school year, we would get together with the kids who went to camp and listen to what they had to say. We just looked at what was working and kept building on that. The kids told us what resonated with them, and we listened. It was pretty simple, really," Tim says.

"Leading by listening," I say. "What a smart way to refine a program. Ask the participants what resonates with them and double down on that. Engagement is actually a simple formula."

"From there it has just taken off," Tim says. "Our program is an incubator. I mean, we're doing stuff that everybody copies."

Tim had lots of training along the way, as well. He attended graduate programs at NYU and was trained in gang mediation, which he applied back home in his Pittsburgh community. But most of all, the dialogue program evolved from listening to the campers from Maine each winter back in Portland as they described what struck them most about their Seeds of Peace experience.

An hour has flown by, and unfortunately, it's time to go. As we prepare to leave, Tim says, "I first met your dad in 1962, at the original Hancock Lumber store there in Casco. They needed a piece of lumber or something at camp, and they sent me to get it. What you're doing is good for you and good for your children. You are leaving a trail of who you are outside of running the business. Lots of people end up running businesses that they never intended to run. Life is funny that way. A business is not *who* you are. You are more than that. This is good for you, and for all of us, the broader stuff you are doing."

I thank him for his kind words, and for sharing so openly with me today. We shake hands on the corner, and he heads down Congress Street toward his home. As I drive west, back toward Casco, I can't help but think how proud Tim's parents would be of him and the formative role they played in his story.

Sometime later, as my Jeep exits the highway ramp in Gray, Simon and Garfunkel's "The Boxer" comes on the radio: "I am just a poor boy, though my story's seldom told…." The timing of the song and its words make me smile. The music combines with Tim's story of the unheralded legacy of Henry and Mamie Wilson, to give me a chill.

> *All lies and jests*
> *Still a man hears what he wants to hear*
> *And disregards the rest*

Henry and Mamie Wilson migrated north to Pittsburgh in 1921 and then worked their entire lives cleaning a steel mill and a hospital. In the process they ended up planting a seed that would go on to help create perhaps the most effective peace camp of our time. You never know the full story of what brings you here. And you often don't know the amazing tale of the inconspicuous person whom you just walked by.

We must learn to listen to ourselves before we can peacefully take in the stories of others. Then we must come to think differently about the fundamental purpose of listening. The purpose of listening is understanding, not judgment. The objective is to allow every person to feel heard and accepted where they are, as they are.

Transcending the need to judge, fix, or correct others is a big leap. Change is tricky. It only comes from within. Seventh Power leaders understand this and consequently make it safe for others to say what they think while resisting the temptation to act on all the information they gather. It's restraint that deepens engagement. It's hearing a different—or even opposing—view without tension or fear. Understanding is contagious. When others feel respected and heard, they enter a new zone of comfort and security. It's here that change becomes possible.

Listening for understanding, not judgment, is the fifth lesson of the age of shared leadership.

CHAPTER 6

Fields of Memory

"Death is the solution to all problems.
No man—no problem."

—JOSEPH STALIN

The odds that Hanna Soroka would survive the winter of 1932 in the Ukraine and live to see her eighth birthday were too small to calculate.

Her parents were dead. Her younger brother and sister were also dead. In fact, in every house Hanna knew, people were dead, and were it not for her nine-year-old sister, Marina, Hanna herself never would have survived.

Hanna was close to death from starvation when pleurisy set in. She had fluid in her lungs, and each breath was a painful chore. Marina, near starvation herself, was by default the head of the family, the oldest surviving member of their once-happy home. Determined to keep her sister alive, Marina built a small fire near the bed and channeled the steam and heat beneath a blanket toward her sister's face.

"It was the steam that saved my life," Hanna would say eighty-four years later, as Alison and I sat in her tiny living room on the eleventh floor of a nondescript Soviet-era apartment complex on the outskirts of Kiev. "Shortly thereafter, someone took me to the hospital on the back of a donkey," Hanna recalls, gesturing with both hands toward our interpreter, Natalie, who is translating from Ukrainian.

"There was no medicine anywhere. The doctor had little hope when he saw me. I could tell he expected me to die," Hanna continues before settling back into her wooden chair, her small blue eyes searching for a confirmation that we understand.

"But I survived," Hanna says defiantly in Ukrainian, looking directly my way. "Stalin and the Bolsheviks tried to kill me, but I survived."

"Sorry, Hanna, I don't understand," I say, patting my chest and then raising my hands to signal confusion.

"Da! Da!" Hanna says with a laugh, nodding and squeezing my hand, remembering Natalie's critical role in the Ukrainian-to-English-translation process.

Hanna's white hair contrasts with the flower-print black dress that falls below her knees. A small white cross hangs from her neck, and her faded wool sweater is unbuttoned and yellowed with age. She wears two pairs of socks but no shoes, the first pair completely covering her legs. The brightest light and the darkest capacities of the human experience are simultaneously illuminated in her remarkable life story.

"My sister was a very strong soul," Hanna continues. Her eyes are wide, and her hands are once again gesturing. "My sister was very organized. She watched the few adults who were left alive and studied what they did. That's how she learned how to keep us alive."

In the spring of 1933 as many as 28,000 Ukrainians were dying of starvation every day on some of the most fertile farmland in all of Europe. That's 1,168 deaths per hour, twenty every minute.

Stalin was likely pleased. In his view, the recalcitrant Ukrainians had been a problem since the onset of Lenin's great socialist revolution. The farmers of the region had not embraced collectivization, nor had they met their grain quotas. Their feisty sense of nationalism was a threat to the entire republic. In Stalin's Union of Soviet Socialist Republics (USSR), there could only be one voice.

Meanwhile, on the docks in Crimea to the south, huge reserves of fresh Ukrainian grain sat waiting for tanker ships to be exported. The Soviets had an industrial revolution to finance, and Ukrainian grain was among their most valued commodities. It turns out, the new Communists were among the most self-serving capitalists on Earth.

Many of the ships pulling into that northern Black Sea port to pick up the grain were British, and a few from the West saw beyond the veil of Soviet propaganda and into the genocide that was occurring. For the most part, however, the outside world knew little of the horrors playing out across the farmlands of the Ukraine.

What happened in 1932 and 1933 would become known by Ukrainians as the Holodomor, or "forced starvation." By the time it was over, somewhere between 4.5 million and 7 million Ukrainians had died of hunger, many in or near their own fields.

"In the end, Stalin lost," Hanna says with a determined single nod as she leans back into her chair. "Stalin is dead, but I'm still here. The Soviet Union is gone, but Ukraine still lives. Stalin could not erase the Ukraine. We are still here."

With that she goes quiet, content that her voice has been heard.

* * *

I FIRST LEARNED ABOUT THE HOLODOMOR accidentally in the spring of 2017—that is, if you believe any life-changing encounter ever happens accidentally. It was a Sunday afternoon. I had just returned from the STAR School in Arizona and was on the couch in my basement scanning television channels for a movie to watch. I had previewed several trailers without much enthusiasm when the movie *Bitter Harvest* caught my eye. The caption read, "When freedom won't be given, it must be taken." *Set against the explosive, war-torn backdrop of 1930s Ukraine, this action-filled epic follows a young artist as he battles famine, imprisonment, and torture to save his childhood love and free his country.*

I pressed PLAY and within minutes I was hooked, riveted by the story as if I were connected somehow (which, of course, we all are). The sensation was similar to the one I had felt five years earlier when I first read about the cultural endurance of the Pine Ridge Indian Reservation in *National Geographic* magazine. Despite sustained and systematic efforts to destroy as many vestiges of Lakota culture as possible, the spirit of Crazy Horse had survived. So, too, did the determined voice of the Ukraine, despite a century-long effort to eradicate it.

I am going to go there, I resolved, when the movie was over. I wondered if there were still survivors, and if so, how I might help to strengthen and preserve their voices.

How had I never heard of the Holodomor? After college I had taught Russian and Soviet history for three years at Bridgton

Academy in Maine. I had even taken some of my students on a tour of the Soviet Union in the spring of 1990. In December of the following year, the USSR dissolved back to its Russian roots.

Nearly twenty-five years later, in the spring of 2014, I found myself watching the nightly news as Russia supported a military insurgency in Eastern Ukraine. This show of force followed the February uprising of the Kiev populace that toppled President Viktor Yanukovych over corruption allegations and his reluctance to strengthen ties with Western Europe. A free Ukraine was now most certainly straying too far for Vladimir Putin's liking. The Ukrainian people were speaking with their own voice, something Moscow had discouraged for a century.

Soon, a rebellion was under way in the eastern region of the country as Russian troops and tanks amassed at the border. The Russian government denied its role in what it described as an organic civil conflict, just as the Soviet regime had denied the existence of a famine in Ukraine eighty-five years earlier. In the Communist Party playbook, the truth is what Moscow says it is. By April the Crimean port region of the Ukraine had been officially annexed by Russia. Message delivered.

Russia is by no means the first or only powerful country to exert influence over a neighbor. Mighty empires have done this for thousands of years. But Russia was overreaching, and lives were being intentionally extinguished for the goals of the capital.

* * *

SINCE THE COLLAPSE OF THE U.S. HOUSING AND MORTGAGE MARKETS in the first decade of the twenty-first century, I have thought a lot about overreaching and the consequences of going too far. Who was responsible for the massive economic collapse that preceded the partial loss of my voice? Pretty much everyone.

A decade earlier President Clinton had decided that increasing home ownership should become a federal objective. Banks were encouraged by the government to find new loan strategies that qualified more people. Lenders then doubled down, stretching the boundaries by creating financial instruments that borrowers (and eventually even bankers) did not understand. Borrowers, for their part, climbed on board. Home builders grew, and lumber companies followed. Everyone was complicit.

A few years later when I began traveling to Pine Ridge, I saw another long shadow of overreaching. The tribes of the northern plains were conquered and colonized in the second half of the nineteenth century as America marched toward its Manifest Destiny. I remember how hollow I felt the first time I realized that genocide had been part of the recipe for America's Western expansion.

The truth is, across human history, those with the most power often go too far. They become self-absorbed and overreach. This is not something that only the Russians or the Americans do. It is something that humans with power do.

What are the defining characteristics of overreaching? While there are many, four surface above the others.

First, there is hubris. The leaders become so entrenched in their roles and their cause that they cannot step back and see the world from any paradigm but their own. When this self-absorbed fog sets, the end suddenly justifies the means.

Second, a sense of shared humanity is lost. The group with the upper hand becomes convinced that their tribe is superior, more valuable. Other groups are expendable, less worthy. Some humans can be sacrificed for the benefit of others. Not all voices matter.

Third, entire populations become complicit by denial. The dark side of the human legacy is uncomfortable, easier to avoid than confront. For example, many Americans would rather just accept the idea that Columbus "discovered a new world" than come to terms with the genocide of millions of indigenous people. With respect to the Holodomor, the Soviets put their propaganda machine to work in the 1930s, and Europe and the Western world chose to stay busy with their own affairs as millions of people died.

Fourth, overreaching has consequences. This is by no means a discovery on one level, as the victims of exploitation feel its impact for generations. But what I mean is, overreaching has consequences for *everyone*, including those who do the overreaching in the first place and, ultimately, for their descendants. Across time, overreaching—be it in business, religion, government, or otherwise—ultimately collapses back upon those who go too far. Whether you are Richard Nixon before Watergate, basketball coach Rick Pitino before the Justice Department crackdown on NCAA recruiting violations, or a lumber company opening too many stores during a boom market, overreaching ultimately undoes those in power.

Those with the most power often go too far. I had done it myself in the run-up to the housing market collapse. We were expanding and spending money and buying companies like we could do no wrong. Along the way, I would use my position of power to ensure that I had the strongest voice.

Then SD came along.

In the contemplation and soul searching that followed, I came to give up what I now describe as the ego-filled mind-set of "global conquest," in which a business sets out to conquer all territory and destroy all competitors.

Today, my frame of reference is quite different. Now I ask, bigger for what purpose, and to whose benefit? Growth is healthy and socially valuable under authentic conditions, but conquerors beware: overreaching invariably collapses back upon those who do it—and they rarely see it coming.

* * *

THE ONLY BRITISH AIRWAYS FLIGHT of the day from London to Kiev is less than half full. Alison sits beside me wearing blue jeans, a faded green denim jacket, and black sneakers. Her blonde ponytail tilts upward as she reads the magazine in her lap.

I glance behind me. Seeing so many empty seats gives me pause. I am excited, but this trip suddenly feels like a stretch. A lumber dealer from Maine traveling to Ukraine to interview survivors of the Holodomor seems, even to me in this moment, like I may be taking it all too far.

But just yesterday I had given a talk at the Osher Lifelong Learning Institute at the University of Southern Maine, where I suggested that "staying in your lane" was a bad idea. What we all need to do, I countered, is intentionally get out of our lane and experience the world in someone else's. I believe that you can learn lots about corporate leadership by stepping beyond the business community and engaging with the world more broadly. The business of business should be bigger than business.

As our plane barrels east on the last Wednesday of September, I reread my most recent email from Yana, the director of the exhibition hall at the Holodomor Victims Memorial in Kiev.

"We are very glad to help you," Yana wrote. "Thank you for your appeal to us and for your interest in this important event. Telling the story of the Holodomor is the only way to prevent such crimes from happening in the future. It is important for humanity to be aware of this great crime that has been hidden for a very long time. Telling the story also makes democracy in Ukraine stronger. The truth is important. It is our pleasure to assist you."

I set down the piece of paper and gaze out the window to my left. Clouds cover whatever lies below as I revisit what I have learned about the story that awaits us.

Ukraine briefly became an independent state in the voids and border reconstructions created during World War I. To the north, against long odds, the Bolshevik Revolution succeeded, and Vladimir Lenin and the Soviets took and held power. When formal establishment of the USSR followed in 1922, Ukraine was folded into the new Communist republic. The new regime in Moscow believed that their revolution would soon usher in a new world order in which the collectivization of economic resources by the state would prevail. In pursuit of this objective, all actions were justified. It was the ultimate play at centralized decision-making and bureaucratic control.

From the beginning, Russian party leaders in Moscow saw Ukrainian nationalism as a threat to the foundation of the Soviet republic. If Ukraine resisted or, worse yet, broke free, other regions might follow.

Joseph Stalin succeeded Lenin as the general secretary of the Central Committee of the Communist Party, and in 1928 he launched the young nation's first "Five-Year Plan." That same year the Communist Party in Moscow initiated its policy of collectivization. All property now officially belonged to the State. Farmers all across the USSR had their homes, horses, pigs, cattle, and land confiscated. Initially, to force local farmers from their homes, the state set quotas for delivering grain. Mandatory requisitions were intentionally established at levels that were impossible to achieve. When the farmers failed to produce, their property was seized. Anyone who resisted, and many who did not, were cast out, imprisoned, exiled, or shot.

Unsurprisingly, grain production across the country plummeted. As the consequences of noncompliance increased and the resources and incentives to harvest crops dwindled, the volume of grain produced further declined. People abandoned their once-fertile fields and fled the region.

But Stalin and his Moscow party bosses were not capable of looking inward. To Stalin, the lack of grain was simply the result of capitalist resistance from wealthy farmers he called "kulaks." Stalin concluded that further intensifying the punishments was the best course, and so the party set out to exterminate any vestiges of resistance. Deportation and death followed.

In 1932, the Soviet Union teetered on the brink of a self-induced collapse due to the lack of bread or food of any sort in the urban centers. In August of that year the Communists invoked what became known in the Ukraine as the "Law of Spikelets." All property was State property, and this applied to every stalk of grain in the fields. Even a woman or a child nearing starvation could be punished severely for taking just a few unauthorized spikelets for themselves.

Stalin was determined to crush the independent voice of the Ukrainian people once and for all. Communists joined criminals and those simply seeking favor with Moscow to further intensify the campaign. Roving gangs of armed marauders traveled from farmhouse to farmhouse, removing every scrap of food, and food source, they could find. Horses, cows, chickens, pigs, and even pets were taken or shot. Kitchens were emptied.

Blockades followed. Desperate farmers and their families tried to flee to the closest city or to another region where a relative resided, but they were turned around and sent back home. International offers of humanitarian aid were rejected. In fact, the very existence of a famine was refuted even as people by the thousands, and then millions, starved.

This was the Ukrainian Holodomor of 1932 and 1933—one of overreaching's finest hours.

* * *

AS OUR PLANE DESCENDS BELOW THE CLOUDS I can see the Dnieper River flowing south to the Black Sea. The sprawling gray mass that is Kiev comes into view.

As Alison and I walk through the airport we see the anticorruption signs posted in both English and Ukrainian. I have never seen such a sign in the United States. While corruption occurs in our country, there is no sense that it will win; despite imperfections, the rule of law prevails. In the Ukraine, however, corruption is pervasive. Corruption is the opposite of democracy. Anywhere democracy is weak or absent, corruption thrives. It's a well-honed form of overreaching.

After collecting our bags and clearing customs, Alison and I find our driver, Yuri, dressed in a black suit. His hair is black but graying, his hands weathered and worn but still strong. He smiles regularly and gestures with animation as he speaks, without regard to the fact that he is driving. He is instantly endearing and eager to share what he knows about the country that he loves.

"Bad times between Russia and Ukraine, bad times," Yuri says, shaking his head, as we approach the large bridge that crosses the Dnieper. On the other side we can see the vast city, home to 3.5 million people. "But it is not the Russian and Ukrainian people who have caused the problems. Bad times caused by the oligarchs—very rich businessmen with political influence. There is no war between the Ukrainian people and the Russian people. For long time the Ukrainian people and the Russian people have lived side by side like brothers."

Yuri pauses for a moment to navigate a lane change. The traffic intensifies as we drive into the city itself.

Yuri's slightly broken English actually enhances communication. His statements are short and to the point, using only the critical words.

"Putin is not president of Russia—Putin is oligarch from Russia," Yuri adds.

Yuri makes me think of Mr. Ali, my friend from Pakistan, whose company buys lumber from our mills in Maine for distribution in his country, and who comes to visit us every year or so. One evening he explained his perspective on the United States. "The people of Pakistan admire and respect America and Americans," Mr. Ali told me. "It's just your government that we don't like, and distrust."

"Corruption is very bad in Ukraine," Yuri continues. "Even driving is corrupt here. That's why we have so many very bad drivers. People pay illegally to get license but don't know how to drive.

"Economy not good, but people still live—people still smile. We are very great optimists, Ukrainian people. And now we are free," Yuri adds, referring to the February 2014 revolution that toppled the pro-Russian government.

"There is corruption in the Ukrainian parliament, of course. But the noose"—he double-checks the word with me in the mirror to make sure it's right before continuing—"the noose is tightening. The people of Ukraine now have control, and we say all the time to our elected officials, if you become corrupt, there will be revolution again and again and again."

The people, not their governmental bureaucracy, are gaining the upper hand.

"Now we have a great friendship with America," Yuri says with a confident smile as we arrive at our hotel. "Trump"—he wrinkles his nose and shakes his head—"not so much, but the American people, very good, very good indeed! Today Ukraine is welcoming the world. If you want to make business, you can make it here. Moscow only thinks about Moscow. We give many thanks to America and Canada for thinking about others besides themselves."

I hope America won't let them down.

As I exit the car I think again about the underlying reason why very few leaders in Washington, DC, or Moscow are effective or popular anymore. It's the system they have volunteered to work in. Federal governments are bastions of central planning in a world that is decentralizing and localizing. It's an old model that hasn't adjusted to the change that is emerging. People want their voice back. People want local flexibility to do what makes sense in their own town and at their own school. It's impossible to set an intimate and inspiring plan for 325 million Americans, or 144 million Russians, from a giant stone office.

"You can't do anything there anymore," our young bartender Ivan tells us later that evening. He's referring to Eastern Ukraine, where the unofficial war with Russia persists. "There is no chance of advancement in that region because there are no jobs, and lots of corruption. Why stay somewhere where there is no opportunity?"

People today are not going to sit in place and be taken advantage of.

Ivan speaks Ukrainian, Russian, and English, and he recently fled the war-torn east in search of work, education, and global connectivity here in Kiev. The opportunity to converse with the rest of the world is what brings him to hotel bartending.

"The conflict in the east is not really a war," Ivan says. "It's all about business. The oligarchs are fighting each other just so they can become richer.

"The people who scream about democracy but do nothing to make the country more democratic—they are not really democratic themselves. They just see government as their chance to be powerful."

"Ivan, have you ever been to the United States?" Alison asks.

Ivan shakes his head.

"It's very hard to go to the US," he replies. "Very few people can get a visa from America. Perhaps one in ten people who would like to go are allowed to visit."

Ivan excuses himself and enters the kitchen to collect an order.

"We have it backwards," Alison says. "We should be encouraging, not discouraging, connectivity."

＊ ＊ ＊

THE HOLODOMOR VICTIMS MEMORIAL is located along a peaceful stretch of park off Lavrska Street overlooking the Dnieper River. It is still early in the morning, and Kiev is only beginning to stir, so we cross the wide boulevard before us easily. The leaves on the hardwood trees are bright yellow, especially brilliant in the rising sun. Ahead, the bells of the memorial tower chime slowly, softly, and methodically. It's quiet otherwise, and we both sense the weight of history. This is sacred ground.

Two stone angels mark the entrance to the memorial. One holds the inscription "1932," and the other "1933." They are known as the Angels of Sorrow, the guardians of the souls of those who died unnecessarily of starvation on some of Europe's most productive farmland.

In the center of the rectangular park is a statue called *Bitter Memory of Childhood*. Here, a young barefoot girl wearing a simple dress looks left with recessed, hollow eyes. Fresh yellow roses are at her feet, testifying that she has not been forgotten. In her right hand she holds five spikelets of grain in recognition of the 1932 law that made it illegal for her to eat them without governmental permission. Although made of bronze, she seems alive.

As we approach the memorial, our guide emerges from the steps below to greet us.

"Hello, I am Natalie. I will be your interpreter for the duration of your stay," she says in clear but methodical English. "You are home here. We are very pleased to have you with us. Thank you for being interested in the story of the Holodomor."

Natalie works for the Memorial. She is thirtyish, with silky brown hair. She wears jeans and a green leather jacket. A brown scarf is wrapped around her neck.

"Please, follow me," Natalie says, gesturing toward the base of the memorial tower itself. "I would like to show you around the grounds before we go into the museum."

The tower is a circular structure overlooking the river, decorated in white and gold. At the base, facing the street, two jagged black rocks jut from the earth; a white stork spirals skyward between them. On the tower itself, four additional storks fly up, away from the earth.

"The storks represent life and the spirits of those who died soaring toward heaven," Natalie explains. "The museum itself is underground," she continues. "This is symbolic, as we are headed back in time, back to the time of the Holodomor."

Together we descend a wide flight of shiny black steps. Inside, at the ticket booth, two elderly women nod their heads and smile as we enter. I am struck with the realization that our visit here is important. Strengthening the voice of this long-repressed act of genocide is still a work in progress.

"The Soviets destroyed as much evidence as possible about the Holodomor," Natalie says, as we stand before a collection of family portraits and farm photographs from the era. "Taking pictures during this period was forbidden by the Communists. The Bolsheviks did not want any record of what was happening. This, therefore, is the mission of our memorial. It is important to prove as fact that this genocide against Ukrainian people occurred."

The central exhibit hall is a circular, dark room with artifacts, photographs, and agricultural tools of the period. In the center, surrounded by white candles, sit the national books of memory containing the names of those who lost their lives. As the bells chime above, Alison and I are invited to each light a small white candle of prayer in honor of the Holodomor. It's a sobering moment. We can feel the reverberations of time and our shared humanity.

"Now, if you are ready," Natalie says, "please come this way and we will sit down and meet Mykola Onyshchanko, our guest of honor and Holodomor survivor."

A few minutes later we are seated on an antiquated cloth couch in a nondescript office at the end of the hall. There is one small window opposite us, high on the wall. Four aged wooden desks fill the room, and a lone computer sits in the back.

Before long, Mykola enters with Yana. We stand to greet everyone, exchanging handshakes, nods, and smiles. Verbal communication is not necessary for this moment to be heartfelt and understood. Everyone knows what brought them here.

Mykola sits opposite me in a small school chair. A table laid with cups of tea and a plate of shortbread cookies separates us. Natalie is at the desk to my right as Yana settles in at the far end of the couch, to my left. Alison sits beside me, iPhone in hand, ready to record our conversation.

I am nervous. I want to get this right, to honor Mykola and his story.

Mykola is healthy, alert, and eager to share. At ninety-two years old, he is surely smaller than he used to be, perhaps five feet five, but fit and strong for his age. He's dressed comfortably, wearing sneakers, gray slacks, and a large blue sweater over a collared shirt. His well-kept white mustache matches his thick eyebrows. His facial features are sharp and distinguished. Born in 1925, he was seven when the horror began.

"Where shall we start?" Natalie asks.

"Let's follow Mykola," I suggest. "We are here to listen. Where would he like to begin?"

Natalie poses this question to Mykola in Ukrainian, and we are off.

"I am glad I can be useful," Mykola begins. "I am here to tell the facts, so that people will know the truth. The truth is important to know so that events like this will not be forgotten or repeated.

"First, I would like to tell you about my family and my life before Holodomor," Mykola says to Natalie, who listens intently, periodically nodding her head with empathy to confirm her understanding as she translates.

"I belonged to a very big family," Mykola continues. "My grandmother, my grandfather, and many relatives, we all lived together, and we were very happy. We lived on a large farm with lots of fields and horses. Life, before the Soviet Union came to Ukraine, before the Bolsheviks came, was beautiful. It was a beautiful village life. We took care of ourselves, and everyone had plenty to eat."

Mykola's description of life before the Soviet Union reminds me of the Lakota on the northern plains before the reservation era.

In both cases, under localized self-rule, the community was happy and healthy.

Mykola speaks with passion. He is determined to be understood. Each time Natalie translates, Mykola looks my way to confirm that I comprehend. Translating Ukrainian to English is not a simple task, and not every word or phrase has a matching counterpart. Natalie is working hard. Everyone is concentrating.

The Ukrainian language is beautiful, even though I don't understand a word. It reminds me of being at Pine Ridge, listening to my friend Verola Spider speak Lakota. In both cases, the act of simply honoring someone else's story fills me with light.

"Then the idea of Communism came to Russia," he says reflectively. "This had horrible consequences." Mykola coughs and pauses to take a drink from a cup of tea on the small table between us.

"After this, life became bad, bad, bad," Mykola says, shaking his head and waving a finger in the air. "The Communists came and took everything. They took all the horses, all the food, everything. Suddenly it was no longer like being a person."

"Who did this, Mykola?" I ask. "Which people came to your village and did this?"

There is lots of back-and-forth as Mykola explains and Natalie confirms.

"These were groups organized by the government, by the Communists," Mykola explains. "Often they were drunkards or idle people who just wanted to win favor with the Communists. They didn't care about other people. They just went from house to house and took everything from the people who had been working harder and living better than them before."

"What happened to those who resisted or fought back?" Alison asks.

Mykola gives a big sigh before closing his eyes and momentarily lowering his head into his hands. We wait quietly, and respectfully.

"Those who resisted in any way were dragged away and put in railcars and sent to Siberia." Mykola's eyes are moist. "Those people were never seen again."

Another pause and another deep sigh.

"When this process was done, there was absolutely no food; not even a single cow remained," Mykola says. "There was nothing to eat. Soon we were all very hungry. At first, especially for a small boy, this all was very confusing.

"I still remember the day it started," Mykola says, taking another deep breath before continuing. "My dad worked at the port and was away. I was home with my mother and sister. Someone came to the house and told my mother that the Communists were coming and taking all the food.

"*What does this mean?* I remember thinking to myself," Mykola says. "No one understood. Why would someone come and take our food? We were not bothering anyone.

"My mother hurried about the kitchen looking for a place to hide the corn and the cucumbers. And then the activists arrived. There were three of them. 'Where is the grain?' they kept asking. My mother said, 'We are not villagers. My husband works at the port; he is not a farmer.' But they did not believe her, and they began looking everywhere. They even looked in the stovepipe, but they didn't find anything. When they left, everyone was crying. This was October of 1932. For us it was the beginning of the Holodomor."

Mykola pauses for more tea.

"By the spring of 1933 it was very, very bad," he continues. "People all around me were dying and doing desperate things because they were so hungry. My mother told us about cannibalism; she would not let us go out in the yard that spring because she was afraid someone might try to eat us. Conditions like these can bring forth horrible acts that would otherwise be unthinkable."

It's impossible to fully comprehend what it felt like at the time, to be there, living this story, as a child.

"People were so thin…so horribly thin," Mykola explains. "They ate everything they had. Most people were barefoot because everybody ate their own leather boots. We ate all the boots in our village. We boiled them into a stew. Everywhere people were swollen with hunger. I saw many people just fall down on the ground and never get back up. It was terrible, just terrible to see."

Mykola pauses.

"I am sorry to ask this question, but what does it feel like to be that hungry, Mykola?" I ask. "How would you describe that feeling to someone who has never known it?"

"It's hard to explain hunger…real hunger," Mykola says. "If you didn't live through this yourself, it's difficult to describe hunger that deep. People lost all their energy and could barely move about.

"I remember walking to school one day and seeing some shit on the ground," Mykola continues. "In that shit was a single kernel of corn. I remember pausing and considering how I might pull out that grain of corn. I was wondering how I would clean it. After all these years I still remember staring down at that single kernel of corn."

I have to take a deep breath. Alison does the same.

"As you sit here today, how do you feel about the future of Ukraine?" I ask.

Natalie begins to ask Mykola the question in English before catching herself. Everybody shares a laugh over this.

"In 2014, the Ukrainian people woke up," Mykola says, referring to what became known as the Revolution of Dignity. "In 2014 the people started to find their own voice and power."

The people started to find their own voice and power. This is the inextinguishable light of humanity, it's the Seventh Power in action, and it's what brings me here to Kiev.

"Can you tell us about your life after the Holodomor?" I ask.

Mykola speaks to Natalie, who then goes over to the computer to check the translation of a word before returning to her seat.

"Mykola went on to work at a very big factory, with 36,000 workers. The factory made locomotive engines and was the biggest in all of the Soviet Union. Mykola was the economic leader of that factory," Natalie explains, pausing to double-check something with Mykola. "Mykola was actually the deputy director of this factory," she says, clarifying. "He says that in the 1970s he went to Moscow to warn the Communist leaders that the Soviet Union could be destroyed. He warned them that the economic system was not functioning properly and that it would collapse if there were no changes. He says he told them this, but no one listened."

"How did you see all of that, Mykola?" I ask, inspired by his foresight. "What made you understand that the entire Soviet system was at risk of collapsing?"

"Who could see this better than I?" Mykola responds. "I was the economist in the factory. I saw all the boo-boos!" Mykola laughs, and then says, "I proposed changes, technology modernizations, and, most importantly, the idea of treating workers differently."

There is a short pause as Mykola and I stretch and change seats. I move the plate of cookies closer to him, and we each take one, smiling and nodding our heads in mutual satisfaction. We are two business executives from very different cultures and eras, celebrating a set of shared core beliefs and two crisp cookies.

"I proposed paying more attention to human rights," Mykola continues once we both have resettled. "I proposed making the people, the workers, more important. We needed to focus on the workers more. We needed to pay attention to their needs, to treat them better. But no one in Moscow would listen to me. The government thought everyone was the same—they were all just workers—but I knew that each person was different. I knew that workers were people first."

"Was it hard to help the same political organization that had done so many bad things to you and your country?" I ask.

Mykola shakes his head and sets his half-eaten cookie back on the white china plate between us. He needs both hands to make his next point.

"No, no, no…it was not hard!" Mykola explains. "I did not care about the government in Moscow. I cared about the people in my factory. I cared about the people in Ukraine. I was trying to make changes to help them, to help the people."

Our time is nearly up, but Mykola shows no signs of tiring, even though we have been in conversation for more than two hours. In fact, it feels as if sharing his story energizes him.

On the floor to my left I pick up a bag filled with small gifts of appreciation that Alison and I have brought for Mykola. One by one I hand him a pine-scented pillow from Hancock Lumber, an L.L. Bean calendar filled with images of Maine, and a jar of blueberry jam from Stonewall Kitchens.

Alison would tell me later that I "way oversold the blueberry jam." This may be true. I was quite excited and lost in the moment. Additionally, if you've ever been in an extended translated discussion, you'll understand how confusing it can get at times. "This is blueberry jam from Maine. Do you know blueberries, Mykola? You spread this on bread or toast. Do you know toast?" Alison insists I said all this much too loudly while simultaneously demonstrating how to spread jam to a man from a country full of bread.

I laugh every time I remember this moment, but by this point, our friendship was real, and I was totally absorbed.

Mykola, the Soviet factory leader from Ukraine, and Kevin, the lumber company executive from Maine, shake hands, smile, and nod again and again in solidarity. It's a moment I don't want to end.

Next, Mykola reaches into his soft leather briefcase and pulls out a collection of pastoral paintings that he has recently completed. He passes around the watercolor depictions of rivers, trees, and fields from his native land.

"They are beautiful, Mykola," Alison says, the rest of us nodding in agreement.

Mykola then returns to his briefcase and extracts a poem he has written about the Holodomor.

"Can you translate this for us, Natalie?" I ask.

Natalie goes to work on her computer and a short while later prints an English version of Mykola's work.

Believe, you can't imagine that
From hunger die these little children.
The one whose face has no image,
Of eyes that saw the death in flesh.
Oh, they can hear, it came for them,
If only there would be some bread.
Did God send judgment for their sins,
Or did Satan pay his visit here?
Some millions died on our land,
On fertile land, my blooming land,
The villages, once full of bread,
Holodomor made your lives end.
The guilty ones were never judged,
Not all was done by us, the living,

To tell the world, so all people know,
Through what survived of our Ukraine.
If our children from the cradle
Did learn about our grief,
And in the churches near the altar,
Holodomor had candlesticks of remembrance.
More than once we all were fooled
By "Older Brother," all along,
So be aware, and stay together.

Mykola's poem momentarily leaves me at a loss for words.

"It's beautiful, Mykola," I say after collecting myself. "May I share this poem with others in hopes that the whole world might someday read your words, and remember?"

"Da! Da!" Mykola responds with a gracious smile, nodding his head.

Just when I think we are ready to go, Mykola has one more story to share.

"I was a prisoner of the Germans in the Second World War," Mykola confides, without feeling the need to elaborate.

What a privilege to meet this amazing man: born just after the Bolshevik takeover of his country, he is a survivor of the Holodomor; he fought for one bully (Stalin) and against another (Hitler); and then he dedicated his career to modernizing and humanizing the very economic system that had tried to systematically kill his entire family. I feel so blessed by this opportunity. No one wants to leave; we all seem to recognize that this is a unique moment, not to be repeated.

"*Djakuyu*, Mykola. *Djakuyu*," I say, clasping his hands and nodding my head. "It was an honor for us to meet you today, and I am pleased that we are now friends. I'm proud to help share your story so that your voice will always be heard. I feel blessed to know you. I feel like we are leaving as friends."

Mykola puts his hands to his heart and nods his head repeatedly. Language is no barrier in this moment.

As we ascend the stairs back into the light, the bells continue to chime. The leaves scatter and dance in the late-morning breeze. We thank Natalie for her invaluable help and retrace our steps across the park.

That night, inside the breathtaking Kiev Opera House, I fall into a peaceful sleep-trance while listening to Mozart's *Requiem*.

Later, as we stroll, my mind wanders back to Mykola.

How could such a hard-edged story of genocide morph into a tale of optimism and a tribute to the human spirit?

Mykola's willingness to share his story reminds me of my dear friend Verola Spider. At her house one fall day, as the rain leaked through her ceiling, she told me stories of her childhood. When she finished she said, "You know, my dad always told us that if we don't share our stories, they die with us."

As we walk along, I think about how fortunate I feel to be here in person and how happy I am to have stepped "outside my lane." Traditional management thinking encourages "staying in your lane" and focusing exclusively on the work of your own company and industry. I don't agree with that axiom of leadership.

When I first started traveling to Pine Ridge and writing, I felt insecure about what others back home would think. The CEO should always be at the grindstone.

But I wanted something different for myself, and for everyone at Hancock Lumber. I wanted work to be balanced and life to be diverse. As productivity expands, work should take less time and energy. In addition, there is as much to be learned away from work as there is within it. Many of my most valuable business ideas have come to me while I am not at Hancock Lumber.

If we stayed at work until there was no more work to do, we would never leave. There's always more that can be done at work, but spending time beyond our confines is the path to growth. I just love it that a lumber company executive from Maine interviewed a Holodomor survivor from Kiev.

* * *

EARLY THE NEXT MORNING Alison and I are standing in front of building #20V on the quiet street known as Prospect Georgiy Gongadze on the outskirts of Kiev.

The edifice is a crumbling Soviet-era apartment complex, symbolic in many ways. It's a gray, twelve-story monolith hanging on in testimony to a bygone era. On the fifth floor an old man in a white sleeveless T-shirt leans out over a concrete portico. Smoking as he looks down, he's most certainly wondering what brings us here.

Soon Natalie and Yana appear, walking our way down the narrow sidewalk. Graffiti covers the trash bins to their left, as well as the abandoned building across the street. We greet each other, and then Natalie places a phone call from her cell phone to Hanna's apartment. Shortly thereafter the red steel door in front of us buzzes and unlocks.

The four of us barely fit in the tiny, herky-jerky elevator. Exposed wires are everywhere as the steel box grinds its way upward, as if making the trip for the final time.

Hanna's daughter meets us in the hallway and welcomes us inside. In the main living area there is a single couch, four wooden chairs, a wooden table, and a Samsung TV. The wall opposite the couch is lined with wooden cabinets with glass doors that reveal a variety of Christian symbols and family collectibles. At the opposite end there is a small balcony filled with plants and a space just large enough to stand in.

Hanna is sitting in a chair near the entrance to the living room. She stands slowly but without assistance.

Once again it feels surreal to be here, recording such a significant voice whose story might not otherwise be known beyond family and friends.

"I was born on February 11, 1925, in central Ukraine," Hanna begins.

"Wait, that's my birthday too!" Alison proclaims with a tilt of her head and a smile. "We are birthday twins!"

Hanna is momentarily confused by the disruption, until Natalie translates. Then an equally exuberant smile overtakes her face, and she begins to laugh. She pats her right leg in celebration, nodding at Alison.

Hanna's voice has a distinct accent. She is alert and animated, clearly committed to preserving the details of her Holodomor experience just as Mykola was.

"I saw many, many people die," Hanna explains. "Both my parents starved to death during the Holodomor. So did my younger brother and sister. Only my older sister and I survived. I remember holding my sister's hand as we walked to the orphanage, because there was no one left alive in our house. I did not want to go to this new house, but they made us go there. There was no food even at the orphanage. How can you have an orphanage without food? After that we ate only grass, flowers, and bark.

"The parents always died first because they saved the food for their children," Hanna continues. "My father was buried in a traditional grave, but I don't remember how my mother was buried when she died a short while later. Neighbors came to our house and said, 'Please, children, go to sleep and do not cry, and do not ask your mother questions; she has gone to sleep for good.'"

"What were your parents' names, Hanna?" I ask.

"Odarka was my mother's name, and Nikifor was my father's name," Hanna replies.

"Hanna, why did you think all of this was happening?" I ask.

Hanna laughs, seemingly at the senselessness of it all.

"It was all so crazy," she replies. "I didn't understand why this was happening. Why did these people come and take everything from us? I didn't understand. I just remember being scared. Every family I knew in my village lost three or more children. In some very big families, everyone died, but at a certain point nobody even came to the houses anymore to collect the bodies or bury the people. Everyone was just so exhausted from starvation. No one could help me or my sister because everyone else was starving too."

As she says this, I glance past her to the picture of the Virgin Mary and Jesus that is taped to the inside of the glass cabinet door opposite me.

"My sister Marina saved my life," Hanna says, before going quiet for a moment, resting her hands in her lap.

"What did your sister look like?" I ask.

"We looked alike, but she was taller," Hanna says with a burst of energy. "I have pictures!"

There is an extended pause in the dialogue as Hanna directs her daughter to the family photo album. For a moment, we are all family reminiscing as images from the past are selected and shared.

"My sister would go on to work all her life on the collective farms," Hanna continues. "She had four sons. Her region was occupied by

Germany during the war. As for me, I was evacuated to the Ural Mountains. This is where the factories for the war were built."

"What are your thoughts on Russia today, Hanna?" I ask.

"First, you must understand that everything that happened to my family when I was young was deliberately organized by Moscow," Hanna says. "Why? Because of only one reason: because we were Ukrainians.

"Why does Moscow not like Ukrainians?" Hanna queries.

We pause, waiting for the punch line.

"Because we drink less and work more," Hanna says with a smile.

We all laugh, and then Hanna goes right back to work.

"When Stalin died [in 1953], everyone cried," Hanna explains. "Why? I didn't cry. I was happy. I was happy, but it was impossible to show your happiness publicly. That would have been dangerous, so I had to keep my happiness hidden."

We all wait patiently for Hanna to continue.

"We are tired of being a part of Moscow," Hanna says directly to me in Ukrainian, waving a defiant finger in the air.

"How do you feel about the future, Hanna?" I ask.

"Better than today," she replies. "I think the future will be better than the past."

Hanna the Holodomor survivor is an optimist. So too is Mykola. I am humbled and inspired.

"Do you think it is important for people to know the real story of the Holodomor?" I ask, intentionally posing an obvious question.

"Of course! Of course!" Hanna says with emphasis. "Why? So such a crime will never again happen. The world should know, because this was a very hard crime on Ukrainian people. It was a crime by the government and everyone should know that. Why would a government intentionally hurt its people? The world must know."

Hanna and I are sitting very close together now, in two of her small wooden chairs with red and blue cushions. We have hit that moment of togetherness when a translator is no longer necessary. We smile, laugh, and hold hands.

"Please tell Hanna I think she is an amazing lady, and that we are honored to be in her home," I say to Natalie. "Please tell her that it makes me happy to be able to hear and share her story." Nodding my head, I say to Hanna, "*Djakuyu.*"

"*Djakuyu, djakuyu*," Hanna replies, folding her hands in her lap. She looks satisfied. Her voice has been heard.

* * *

THAT AFTERNOON ALISON AND I VISIT THE GROUNDS at Saint Sophia's Cathedral. Inside a blue and gold dome-topped building near the center of this eleventh-century bastion of Christian orthodoxy is an exhibit dedicated to the pursuit of leadership restraint. The collection of pictures and documents commemorates a comprehensive essay titled "New Chronicle and Good Government." It was written in Peru by Felipe Guaman Poma de Ayala over four hundred years ago. The 1,200-page manuscript is addressed to King Philip III of Spain, but the exhibit explains that there is no evidence that he ever received its wisdom.

The central poster in the middle of the room reads:

> *In good government the author depicts the injustice, exploitation, and abuse of power of colonial rule, and also offers suggestions to the Spanish crown for governmental reform in Spain's new colonies.*

The book itself went missing for hundreds of years before it was discovered in a Copenhagen library in 1918. His writing was just as relevant in 1918 as it was in 1615. The Western world today is still living with the consequence of colonization (another extreme example of overreaching).

* * *

LATER THAT EVENING ALISON AND I are in a taxi headed for dinner. Cher is singing on the radio as fuzzy dice and a Jesus Christ figurine swing from the rearview mirror.

"I have lived my entire life in Kiev," our driver, Artem, says. "But now all the names of the streets are changing. Any street with a Communist name, they are taking it down, giving the streets new names.

"Music OK?" Artem asks, gesturing to the radio, which is tuned to 103.6 FM, Radio ROKS Kiev.

"Yes, it's great," Alison replies.

"OK, good," Artem responds, nodding. "I was born in the Soviet Union, but I love rock and roll. Growing up, it was hard to listen to the music that I liked. The Communists tried everything to take away our music because they did not want any influence from the West."

"Where did you live in the Soviet Union?" I ask, momentarily confused.

"Right here," Artem replies, surprised by my question. "Right here," he repeats. "The Soviet Union came to Kiev."

"Ah, right," I acknowledge, leaning back into my seat and feeling a bit silly.

The Soviet Union came to Kiev with a heavy hand, just as America came to the land of Crazy Horse in the second half of the nineteenth century. Both were sure they were in the right. Those who hold the most power often overreach. They go too far, and this has consequences.

Kiev's view of Russia today is shaped by Soviet and Russian overreaching. Some might in turn say that Russian overreaching was driven by Western imperialism. Did the capitalists or the Communists overreach? The answer is yes and yes. Restricting the personal power of others is almost always done in the name of protecting the personal power of others. While ironic, in all cases it has consequences. From Kiev to Pine Ridge, you can see the vestiges of going too far.

Restraint is the opposite of overreaching. It's having the power but not using it. Restraint, not force, is the new path to building consensus, alignment, and engagement.

This is the sixth lesson of the age of shared leadership.

CHAPTER 7

From the Ashes

"The world as we have created it is a process of our thinking.
It cannot be changed without changing our thinking."

—ALBERT EINSTEIN

"The idea of creating a new normal permeates everything we do," Pankaj Srivastava explains.

Pankaj is from India, but he is speaking to me from his home in San Francisco while serving as the COO of an inspiring Ukrainian technology company called ZEO Alliance (ZEO). In 2010 Slava Kolomeichuk and Yuriy Dvoinos launched MacKeeper, an all-in-one platform for Apple Computer users. Today, that product has over twenty-five million installs in eighteen languages. The success of MacKeeper led to the creation of ZEO Alliance, a technology company driven by a culture of shared leadership. ZEO aspires to change the world through innovation. Today, from their head-quarters in Kiev, they attract young thinkers and aspiring product developers from across Ukraine.

Though ZEO's products are numerous and interesting, it's the purpose-driven nature of the organization that attracted my attention. The mission of ZEO Alliance demonstrates how modern corporations can transcend tribalism, collaborate cross-culturally, and make advancing the human condition the primary goal.

It's a few weeks before my trip to Kiev, and Pankaj and I are speaking by telephone about the audacious social goals that drive the company he serves.

"What do you mean by 'creating a new normal,' Pankaj?" I ask.

"A new normal is something—anything, really—that allows us to accelerate the evolution of humans through inspired purpose, education, and empowerment," Pankaj says.

"We don't believe in top-down at all," Pankaj continues. "We believe in shared responsibility. Everyone must be engaged and involved in the process of creating a new normal. It's really all about trust—trusting the people around you, and sharing responsibility and opportunity equally.

"As each individual on Earth moves closer to their potential, all of humanity is advanced. That's what we are about as a company: helping people develop their own unique skills and voice. Everything we do should create a new standard for something. It should make the world better in some small way. Otherwise, what's the point?"

"I'm inspired by this enlightened view of your company's purpose," I say. "Corporations have developed a reputation for being self-absorbed with their own internal goals. Yet here you are, adopting the corporate mission of improving the world. How do you go about advancing such a lofty cause while still achieving operational focus and performance excellence?"

"It's all about creating a culture where everyone is invited to lead," Pankaj says.

This statement causes me to pause. It's the exact same objective we are pursuing at a lumber company in Maine. It reminds me of the age-old human question: was fire invented once, or multiple times, across a variety of disconnected tribes?

"When everyone leads, both the corporation and the individuals within it grow," Pankaj says. "In this way, humanity advances. It's all about putting people first. Take, for example, a simple business discussion. At ZEO, the objective of a discussion is learning. Discussions are not designed to tell, teach, or make money. Our first move in any conversation is to simply ask others what they think. The goal is always to build confidence in others.

"When I ask the question 'What do you think?' it strengthens the person I am talking to. It sends an important signal that their opinion is valuable. People begin thinking to themselves, 'I must have something to offer if the leaders of this organization are asking me questions.'"

Pankaj has me thinking about my own response to spasmodic dysphonia and the power of leaders asking questions rather than giving answers. In the years following the onset of SD, time and again it struck me that the person I was listening to already had great answers to their own questions; they already knew what to do. They didn't actually need a CEO-centric solution; all they needed was someone to encourage them to trust themselves. SD, I came to realize, was a power-dispersing disorder.

"When you look at people who become really successful, you will see that they have lots of followers," Pankaj continues. "Success does not necessarily mean that someone makes a bunch of money. Success, really, is defined by the followers you acquire by virtue of the ideas you share and the values you live by."

Stalin coerced loyalty, whereas Pankaj and the ZEO team understand that true followership is voluntary.

"I learned from my dad, only after he died, that looking at followers is a better way to measure success than calculating wealth or material possessions," Pankaj says. "I grew up Hindu in India, where it's customary for the eldest son to lead the funeral parade for his father. The day came when my father passed, and there I was, walking in front of the procession. Behind me four people were shouldering my father's body as we walked through our neighborhood in Bombay. Suddenly I sensed this amazing crowd behind me, so I turned around and looked back."

Pankaj pauses.

"There were over two thousand people in that parade, from all walks of life: cabinet ministers and janitors alike were there, walking, paying respect to my dad. My dad grew up in a poverty-stricken household and became an engineer. He was never famous on a wide level, but lots of people admired and respected him and his wisdom. He was rich in followers. This is when I realized the true definition of success.

"So today, when I think about success, I think of voluntary followers. That's what ZEO is about. Sure, we have a profit motive, and that's important, but we also have a motive of sharing and giving to others, just because it's the right thing to do. Take ZEO University, for example: Here we bring in talented people and give them a free education with no obligation on the student's part to do anything for us in return. Occasionally someone will graduate from our training program and join a direct competitor. We don't mind that. In fact, we celebrate it, because our big goal is to build human capacity."

ZEO is less than a decade old, but already its business model is thriving, with more than 1,400 employees and a rapidly growing list of successful products and services that are competing on a global scale.

"I love the idea that followership is voluntary, and perhaps the best possible indicator of success," I say. "How does it feel to be spreading this wisdom in a region where followership was often driven by coercion, and the truth centrally planned? Is this a big transition for the young people within your company?"

"What I sense from the young generation in Kiev is that they don't dwell on the past legacy of their country," Pankaj replies. "They are more focused on how to create their own new energy. The new generation in the Ukraine is ready for remarkable change. They have moved past the Soviet-era style of thinking and leadership.

"Don't get me wrong," he continues. "There are some geopolitical tensions that are pulling them back. For example, the Ukraine still has a lot of the old USSR corruption in its system, and people will be dealing with that for some time, but that is not stopping them. They are finding ways to engage and compete and express themselves on a global stage. The closer to Poland you get, the faster it all is changing. People are more exposed to freedom the farther west you go. But everywhere in Kiev, people are embracing the opportunity to speak with their own true voice. At ZEO we want to accelerate that change by encouraging everyone to express themselves authentically."

"What's the one big idea that makes it all work?" I ask.

"It's simply that everybody has value," Pankaj says. "Everybody has important ideas. Our culture is designed to share leadership broadly, with everyone we meet."

* * *

You can't get a Diet Coke in Kiev.

I mean, perhaps technically you can find one somewhere in this sprawling granite city, but trust me, it's not worth the search.

For the third day in a row I climbed Bohdana Khmel'nyts'koho Street to the point where it crests in front of the National Opera House in search of my favorite soft drink, and for the third day in a row I was denied. *Old habits die hard*, I think, turning around to begin my descent back to the hotel.

It's the morning after our visits with Mykola and Hanna, and as I walk, my mind is with them and the conditions that caused such unimaginable and unnecessary human suffering. How are such calculated and vast atrocities sustained? How could a small group of individuals at the center tip an entire culture into allowing such callousness to reign? And to what end? The Holodomor is an extreme example of what can happen when the capital becomes obsessed with its own self-serving objectives. Millions of humans were sacrificed so that the success of the center might be advanced.

From a distance, it's easy to see the absurdity of it all. An organization can never win in the end through exploitation and destruction. Nor can an organization thrive by becoming self-absorbed.

Stepping back, it seems partly heartwarming, partly obsessive. I have just become highly sensitized to the story of leaders restricting the free voices of others. Furthermore, I believe the leaders of today can reverse these broken patterns. We can break the momentum. But to do this, leaders must work beyond the narrow confines of their chosen industry.

I could spend sixty-five hours a week at work, but this would not make me a better human or a better manager. The purpose of work is to support, not thwart, the meaning of life. Companies must create pay systems, work schedules, and human missions that put time back in the hands of employees. The objective is to help everyone get out of their lane and broaden their lives.

I call this "putting the work back in its place." It's about making the work exciting and important, but not all-consuming. As productivity expands, work should take less time. Sure, we can use some of our productivity achievements to make more lumber and deliver more building materials. But how about also using some of the freed capacity to just plain work less?

The fresh idea is to select corporate goals that also directly improve the lives of the people doing the work. In 2012, the same year I began traveling to Pine Ridge, Hancock Lumber launched an initiative to make sure our delivery trucks were "full and freighted" when they left the yard. To accomplish this, we began tracking a simple metric we now call *journey value*. Journey value calculates the total value of all the products on a truck as it embarks on a round of deliveries. We asked our customers, sellers, and logistics managers to share responsibility for driving this metric. In the five years that followed, we doubled our sales, but the number of deliveries we made actually went down. In 2017, on double the sales, we had more capacity than we did in 2012, without adding a single truck to the fleet. (Although we purchased a good number of new vehicles during this period, the size of the fleet did not expand.)

During this period, we set the goal of reducing the average hourly workweek in our stores from forty-seven to forty. To do this, we had to take on some long-entrenched corporate monuments, such as overtime pay. The overtime pay system is the worst possible compensation system for the modern age, as you earn more money the longer the work takes. A progressive pay system does just the opposite: It incentivizes individuals and teams to make the work more accurate, more efficient, and less time-consuming. As the work takes less time, both the employees and the company earn more.

To implement this, we raised base pay levels and added new bonus incentives that paid on safety, accuracy, and efficiency. Soon, our employees were making more money working forty hours a week than they had when they were working forty-seven. This is human capacity freed.

Multiply seven fewer hours a week at work by forty-eight weeks of work per year, and you have 336 hours that can be redeployed. Across a thirty-year work career, that's more than ten thousand hours of human capacity. Multiplied again exponentially across our 525 employees, that's over 5.2 million hours—freed by Hancock Lumber alone.

I have become a proponent of encouraging people to get out of their lane. The boss was traditionally someone who may have expected others to be all about their work, commending them for coming in early and staying late. Of course, there will be times when employees need to go into overdrive for the company, but that should not be the normative state. The purpose of the company is to enhance the lives of the people who work there. My wish is for our company is to become so accurate and efficient that the work takes less time. This allows everyone to expand their connectivity and share their energy more broadly.

Corporations—and nations—can no longer stay in their bubble and expect the rest of the world to be just fine. Every person's story is personal and collective, pouring into the narrative of our shared human journey. That's why your neighbor matters. That's why *you* matter. What happens to one happens to all. The broader the corporate mission, the better. Companies in the twenty-first century have an unprecedented opportunity to free human capacity and send it forth into the larger world.

* * *

Victoria Strokan, ZEO's communications director, meets us in the lobby. A friendly robot opposite the reception desk is also part of the welcoming committee.

A modern techno decor of steel and wire surrounds us. We receive our electronic passes, swipe them at the sleek metallic entry system, and enter ZEO's compound. Everywhere we turn the indicators of free expression are in the air.

Culture matters, I think, as we tour the bright and colorful spaces that contrast dramatically with the distant images of the monolithic halls of government in Kiev, Moscow, or DC.

"ZEO is a place where people can relax, be themselves, explore, and grow," Victoria says as we pass through a cafeteria on one of the upper floors.

Victoria is full of passion for her company and its mission.

"Everyone here is encouraged to devote twenty percent of their time to side projects, to their own ideas for new products and services," she says. "Our culture is full of idea-sharing opportunities. There is lots of listening here too, lots of surveys designed to make the voices of our associates strong. People ask lots of questions, especially our leaders. Our leaders do more asking and listening than explaining or telling. Our strength as a company is that the people here are heard."

What a contrast to the Soviet model of leadership, with its single voice. ZEO feels more like a place to live than a place to work. There are huddle pods for small gatherings, dance studios, places to rest, and places to recreate. Every room is a colorful, modern space of inspiration.

"Today we have arranged for five of our project team leaders to meet with you," Victoria says as she escorts us into a room filled with beanbag chairs and foam pillows.

The door closes, and a few moments later a young man knocks and enters with a warm smile.

"Hello, I am Serge," he says.

Serge is perhaps thirty, comfortably dressed in blue jeans, a blue sweater, and sandals over thick wool socks. Earbuds hang loosely from his shoulders.

"How has Ukraine changed since independence?" I ask.

Serge leans forward a bit, adjusting his position in the red beanbag chair.

"I was five years old when Ukraine gained its independence," he says. "From my perspective it was just a matter of time before the Soviet Union collapsed. When a country—or any organization—is built on lies, it's on borrowed time until the truth gets back to the people. The era of the Soviet Union in Kiev was a time of zombies. People were not thinking. But give the Soviets credit: they did a great job making people not pay attention to what was really happening around them.

"We are moving on. We are engaging the world. There are lots of exciting opportunities for young people in our country who wish to learn and be creative."

"What's the culture like here at ZEO?" I ask.

"ZEO is a place that allows someone like me to connect with the world and test new ideas. It's a place where we can think, experiment, and create."

"Is there one word that best defines ZEO?" I ask.

Serge pauses.

"Safe," he says. "It's safe here."

"What do you mean by that?" I ask.

"I can be myself here," Serge says. "The culture of the company makes it safe for all of us to just be ourselves. We can dress as we like. We can schedule our time as we like. Most importantly, we can say what we like. ZEO is a place that encourages authenticity. People here are free to speak with their own voice. This is very powerful. Our loyalty to the company is strong because of the opportunities it creates for us as individuals."

As Serge departs Nick enters the room, wearing a Stanford football cap and a Nike T-shirt.

Nick was born in 1991, just six days before his country's independence and the same year I started working at Hancock Lumber. He is a child of post-Soviet Ukraine, and no stranger to America, having spent a foreign-exchange year in Idaho, as well as a summer in Washington, DC.

"I am from Western Ukraine, near Poland," Nick says. "I have personally witnessed the cultures of East and West merging and coming closer together for some time. In 2008 I spent a year in America; there was Facebook and YouTube in the United States, but not in the Ukraine. So when I came back home, it felt very different here. But today, just a decade later, there is no technology lag. We can see the whole world from Kiev, and this makes it much more difficult for a totalitarian regime, or any small group of people, to hide the truth from everyone."

"What does totalitarianism mean to you?" I ask.

"In a totalitarian society everything is planned and watched by the center," Nick says. "It's a place where you need a permit to make even basic travel plans, or to do anything of significance. It's a place where the whole country is managed by the center of government. But it's changing fast right now. The Ukrainian Communist Party did not win a single seat in Parliament in the last election. Their vote was less than five percent. That's a huge change in just a generation—from all the seats to none of the seats. But still, there are the politicians, the oligarchs. An oligarch is a person that is just in it for the power, the fame, and the money, without any vision."

"What's the biggest problem facing modern-day Ukraine?" I ask.

"Ukraine has only one big problem, and that is corruption," Nick says without hesitation. "Unfair courts and corruption are our biggest challenges as a nation. It's everywhere, and it's sad. As a young person, I would never bribe someone. I do not want to give that kind of country to my kids.

"Did you know that corruption in the Ukraine is like sport fishing in America?"

"No. I did not know that," I reply, playing my part.

"You catch a fish, take a picture, and then release the fish," Nick says. "It is catch-and-release, just like the way our country traditionally handles corruption. In the end I am not worried about Russia or any other country. It's more about Ukraine not messing up its own future. We always have to look first at ourselves. We respect Russia and all other countries. We just want our own voice and identity in return."

There is a knock at the door.

Vladimir enters, wearing a plain white T-shirt with a black outline that looks like a Rorschach inkblot test.

"It's a bat," Vladimir says, anticipating my question as he sits down. "I am a big fan of Batman."

Vladimir looks like he could play the part of Robin, the Boy Wonder, fit, with long arms, short hair, youthful energy, and a quick wit.

"You are from Maine, correct?" Vladimir says.

"Yes, we are," I reply.

"I spent a summer there in 2008 working at this amusement park in Saco called Funtown Splashtown USA," he says.

"What? Wait!" I reply. "We used to take our daughters and their friends there every summer. You probably collected my inner tube or told me it was my turn on the slide. What a small world!"

"I probably did," Vladimir says with a smile. "What I like about your country is that people who really want to work will find a job, build a career, and make a living. In Ukraine today people do not have that same opportunity. Even if we have a job, for many of us the pay is so small that you cannot afford to buy anything. We are very lucky here at ZEO, because it represents something different. I am fortunate."

"Did anything else strike you about America?" I ask.

"Yes, it's simple in the best sense," Vladimir says. "By this I mean not fancy. Ukraine is fancy and showy. In America you can be a very rich person yet still humble, friendly, kind, ordinary—normal and not pretentious. Seeing that made a very big impression on me. It actually made a shift in my brain—that success is not about showing off."

"What's it like here at ZEO?" I ask.

"Open-minded," Vladimir says without hesitation. "The leaders are very interested in the ideas of others. Also, they are very flexible in their approach to work. Each person here has the freedom to be innovative and creative.

"There is very little bureaucracy here. I'm a general manager, but typically I'm just out there working with the team."

"How does the culture of the company help produce great results?" I ask.

"It's not corrupt here," Vladimir says. "It's not slow. Giving people freedom improves results. Everyone is treated as important. This is a place where people can grow. In return, people create great work that strengthens the company. The people come first here."

Dimitry is next into the room. After our greeting he grabs a beanbag chair and pulls it forward, revealing the phrase RELAX MORE painted on the floor.

"ZEO is an idea hub," Dimitry says, opening the conversation.

The son of a Polish mom and Russian dad, Dimitry has led the development of a Kindle-type device for reading books electronically that is very popular in Eastern Europe, Russia, and China.

"Look at it," he says with pride, handing one forward. "It's the fastest, brightest, and smallest unit on the market today. It's called the 'Pocket Book' because it fits in your back pocket.

"We are transitioning from outsourcing to creating for ourselves," Dimitry says. "In the early years after independence the engineers in Ukraine represented huge margins for Western technology companies that sold our services. They would sell our work time for fifty dollars per hour and pay us three hundred dollars per month. But Ukraine is transitioning, and we are now creating for ourselves. That's what we do here at ZEO. We keep the development value of our own work right here in the Ukraine, and we do it with very little hierarchy."

"How are your work teams organized?" I ask.

"There are thirty people on the team that I belong to," Dimitry says. "We have no vertical structure here. The teams are flexible, and they change with demand. Everyone can bring important ideas forward; even the person who cleans the floors participates in our idea-sharing processes. Every voice here matters."

Alina is the last ZEO leader of the day to join us.

"What is it like working at ZEO?" I ask.

"It's confidence building," Alina replies. "This is a place where we all have come to see that we can compete globally."

"Can you tell me more about that?" I ask.

"Just because someone looks experienced, or British, say, or in their fifties, none of that means they are smarter than you," Alina says. "Once I had the opportunity to get out into the world, I could see this, and it gave me confidence for the people of Ukraine. How would we stack up? Until recently this was a question we could only wonder about. Now we know. We can do this. We can compete and add value globally. It's a very exciting time for us."

Great people are everywhere, I think. It's the culture that makes the difference.

"How would you describe the culture at ZEO?" I ask.

"I have worked in both the old and new corporate environ-ments, and there is a very big difference," Alina says. "The old environment was all about working under pressure. It was very results driven, very tough on each other, person to person. The leaders created even more pressure, intentionally, between people and work teams."

Alina pauses and laughs, seemingly at the absurdity of it all.

"That's OK for some, I guess," she continues. "But I just felt like it was unsustainable. It wasn't for me. It wasn't something that I wanted to be a part of.

"Here at ZEO the culture is open and encouraging. You want to do well not because of your boss, or even because they pay you. You just really want to do well because you are excited about what you are doing, and the group you do it with. So basically I learned how to be a good leader by seeing what people were doing wrong in the old system."

"It must be exciting to be part of all the innovation that is created here," I say.

"Growing up I was always a bit of a rebel against the existing order," Alina says. "I guess I was meant to help reinvent things. I was always disagreeing with what my parents and teachers and bosses were trying to put into me. I was, like, who are you to tell me how to think?

"We all have our own truth," Alina continues. "There is no absolute truth. We all are here to express what we think and then to listen to others, and then, maybe then, you find a third truth, which is better than either truth before."

"What is the organizational structure like at ZEO?" I say.

"We have a very flat structure. As a result, we have the ability to be open and honest with everyone—even the CEO. When the bosses can listen and be wrong and hear the opinions of others, that is how they show they are strong. It's like what Margaret Thatcher once said: power is like being a lady—if you have to tell people you are, you aren't.

"It feels free to me here. I like being at ZEO because I like myself when I work here. In my last job I didn't like myself. Here I am always telling people they are amazing. That's such an energizing thing to do."

What a great way to think about work: do you like yourself when you go there?

The door opens, and Victoria peers in. Our afternoon within ZEO's inspiring confines is just about over. Everything Pankaj described to me on the phone from his office in San Francisco has come to life here this afternoon.

ZEO is achieving excellence within its field of expertise by expanding its mission. ZEO exists to advance humanity. Technological innovation is a path to a larger purpose.

For a long time, leaders were encouraged to narrow their focus and drive incremental change by putting all their energy into their production line or core business processes. Of course, this is important work, but it has its limits.

Making faster, better widgets should not be the sole purpose of any company. Using technology and modern, lean operating systems does free up human capacity. Some of that capacity can be used to make more products and provide more services. But what if some of that capacity was actually used to just plain work less?

As work becomes more accurate and efficient, work should take less time. As work takes less time, human lives become more balanced and diversified. As this happens, connectivity and awareness grow.

In the modern age, a lumber company executive from Maine should be spending time on the Pine Ridge Indian Reservation and interviewing Holodomor survivors and technology superstars in Kiev.

* * *

The following morning Alison and I are back at Kiev's Boryspil International Airport. The anticorruption signs catch my attention in a more meaningful way as we leave. Corruption is overreaching. It's those who already hold the most power going too far.

Our day at ZEO has me thinking: The company is walking a delicate line as it endeavors to change its country and region from within. ZEO comes from a place where corruption is normal and totalitarianism expected. Yet, there is no animosity or anger to be found. ZEO is engaging Russia and other Eastern European markets with respect and fresh eyes. It's a perspective I felt many times in Kiev.

Russia's power could grow exponentially in this region simply by learning to respect the independent voices of others. To do this, Russia would first need to look within itself and confront its past, making peace from within and realizing its own inherent beauty and Seventh Power capabilities. Russia doesn't need intimidation and force to be respected, valued, trusted, and heard. While this is a hard transformation for those already in power to undertake, it's what must occur. Those who hold power must become more self-aware and then dare to make the transition from overreaching to restraint.

In my small backpack rests a crisp blue-and-yellow Ukrainian national flag.

"If they ask me at customs if I have anything to declare, I am going to declare my affection for the Ukrainian people. Freedom is fresh here. Connectivity is respected. None of it is taken for granted," I say as we wait for the red light at the checkpoint in front of us to turn green.

The human voice is a hard thing to keep down. Despite generations of totalitarianism, free voices abound in Kiev, and ZEO is leading the way.

As Pankaj explained, "We are committed to creating a new normal. We support any activity that accelerates the evolution of humans through inspired purpose."

The leaders at ZEO have created a culture where every voice is safe, respected, and heard—a world-class company built on the premise of leadership restraint. The leaders at ZEO are charmingly hard to find. They wear blue jeans and sneakers, and they blend into the crowd. They are *in* the circle, not above it, asking questions rather than dictating answers. They are serving others, not being served. The individual quest for authentic self-expression is a candle that cannot be extinguished. You can find this truth anywhere on Earth, including in Kiev.

But I also find ZEO inspiring in a way that some might overlook. ZEO has expanded its mission to include all of humanity. For business cultures to evolve, they must transcend the false premise that a company is all about value creation for shareholders. That's a self-centered idea in a world that is transitioning toward authentic service to others.

Of course, shareholder value matters. But for me, it's more of an outcome than a goal. If the company creates a culture that serves employees and improves their lives, the company will be cared for and respected in return.

I recently heard Harvard Business School professor Rebecca Henderson give a talk titled "Reimagining Capitalism." In her remarks, she explained why governments were increasingly going to have difficulty solving society's most complex problems. Instead, she advocated for a rebirth of localism and called upon individual companies to view their mission more broadly. If every company embraced heightened environmentalism, health-care transparency, and wage stagnation, the scales would eventually tip.

Corporations are trained to be agile problem solvers. The transition required is to take those skills and use them broadly, for the benefit of all of society. In the old world order it would be hard to explain why a lumber company CEO from Maine is in Kiev interviewing Holodomor survivors. In the new world order it would be hard to explain why I'm just staying at home, focused on my own narrow needs.

* * *

A LONDON CAB IS AN INSTITUTION UNTO ITSELF. It's only expensive if you consider it to be just a ride.

Our black cab, slender yet tall at the center, weaves through London traffic with ease as our driver drifts adroitly in and out of our conversation. To our left the green fields and giant hardwood trees of Kensington Gardens come into view. Bikers and walkers, dogs and geese, all take their place in this the timeless British scene.

A short while later, Alison and I arrive outside Cecconi's Mayfair restaurant at 5A Burlington Gardens. As we exit onto the narrow, winding street, the cranes above are churning in their restoration assignment at the Royal Academy of Arts. Men and women in overcoats make their way to work, umbrella in one hand, coffee in the other, earbuds deployed.

Inside Cecconi's, young men and women in crisp white shirts, black vests, and bow ties distribute the accoutrements of a traditional English breakfast. At a white table with green leather chairs to the right of the central bar, I spot the man we have come to see, Jose Miguel Sokoloff.

I first learned of Jose and his work months ago, while watching *60 Minutes*.

"For more than half a century, Colombia was one of the most violent and isolated countries on Earth," Lara Logan reported, opening a segment titled "How Unconventional Thinking Transformed a War-Torn Colombia."

"Infamous for cartels, cocaine, and kidnapping, the Revolutionary Armed Forces of Colombia [in Spanish, *Las Fuerzas Armadas Revolucionarias de Colombia*, or FARC] fought the government in the longest-running war in the Western Hemisphere—until recently," Lara said, "when Colombia achieved what many thought was impossible. How do you end a fifty-two-year war that left 220,000 dead and millions displaced?

"The Colombian military came up with one of the most unusual ideas in modern warfare: an advertising campaign. They hired a creative ad executive, Jose Miguel Sokoloff, to convince thousands of fighters to give up without firing a shot," Lara says. "How did Sokoloff do it? With soccer balls and Christmas trees."

The story immediately struck me as the type of fresh leadership I was searching for. Listening to an enemy during war, as a means to end war, was inspiring work. So I pressed PAUSE on the remote and raced into my office for Evan's notebook, sliding to a stop in my socks on the wooden floor beside my desk. "I'm going to meet him," I said to myself when the segment ended.

"Thank you for making this time for us," I say after we have taken a seat at his side.

Jose smiles graciously.

"Where would you like to begin?" he asks.

"Wherever you think is best," I say. "I'm interested in hearing this story from your perspective, as you experienced it."

"Very well, then," Jose says. "Let's start at the end."

Jose's hair is short, a distinguished mix of gray and black, framing his handsome, tan face and large black glasses. He is comfortably dressed in blue jeans and a black sweater. He speaks softly yet confidently, a thinker who's willing to share.

"During the negotiations in 2016 the guerrilla bosses at the table insisted that the marketing campaign we launched [to encourage rebels to demobilize] be stopped as a condition of any continuation in the peace talks," Jose explains. "This proved to me that the messaging campaign worked, and that the guerrillas had no way to combat it."

"What were the origins of the guerrilla war in the first place?" I ask. "How did the conflict start?"

"At the end of the nineteenth century, Colombia had two factions that opposed each other in what became known as the 'War of a Thousand Days,'" Jose replies. "This war was between those who wanted the church at the center of the state and those who did not. The liberal forces won out, and this created a lot of displacement, as many of the large agricultural landowners were forced to abandon their property and move to the cities. But in the late 1950s the tables turned, and the conservatives gained power. They pledged to restore the original land ownership rights of those who were displaced. This turned into a battle with the peasants, who

204 ■ THE SEVENTH POWER

now occupied the land, so then the military came in and started forcibly removing people from their homes and fields. This was the beginning of FARC, the Revolutionary Armed Forces of Colombia."

Overreaching and unilateralism cut both ways. In a predictable pattern, one side gains the upper hand and exploits the other. Eventually the tide turns, and the opposite side exacts revenge. Like a seesaw on the playground, each injury incites the next. Kings and capitalists, communists and revolutionaries, Christians, Jews, and Muslims—they all overreach. Revolutionaries are born from discontent, but often soon become corrupt themselves. Two sides, each injured by the other, take turns going too far. This is a story without borders, a broken pattern that belongs to everyone.

I have been thinking a lot about unilateralism back home. Our country is full of good examples. Whichever political party in Congress has one more vote than the other runs the table. The Democrats had done this in partnership with President Obama to rewrite health-care law; now the Republicans had done the same with tax reform. Policy without consensus creates distrust, division, and revenge. Overreaching always has consequences.

I have learned this same lesson the hard way within my own company. As the CEO I have the power to push initiatives through the organization, but that doesn't mean I should. Typically, when I unilaterally impose a decision, it fails. Ultimately, there is a price to pay for moving without consensus. Occasionally, at a pivotal moment where decisive action is required, it may be necessary, but in normal times patience for process prevails.

"So that is how the guerrilla movement started," Jose says. "But then things began to change. In the 1960s, the Communists in Cuba became increasingly active all across South America. At that point, FARC essentially became funded by the Soviet Union.

they evolved to become exploiters themselves, taking advantage of the very people they had banded together to protect. It happens whenever greed creeps in and the leaders put the organization before the people it was created to serve.

"So then spring arrived and the qualifying tournament for the World Cup came along," Jose says. "We already knew through our interviews that the guerrillas love soccer and went out of their way to find ways to listen to or watch the games. This was a special year because Colombia had a very strong team. The entire country was energized and excited to see Colombia compete and qualify for the World Cup. So we decided to invite the guerrillas to come home once again—this time, to watch soccer. Our national team was something that united the country and transcended the war. In the weeks leading up to the competition we began dropping soccer balls into the jungle with little messages attached, inviting the guerrillas to come home and watch the games. As the games themselves began, we also honored and welcomed home former guerrillas at halftime. This was our most successful campaign. Eight hundred rebels came home. At the time the guerrilla leaders said they had twelve thousand to fifteen thousand men, but our estimate was that they had perhaps five to six thousand fighters left, so eight hundred demobilizations was a lot."

"So what is the status of the war today?" I ask. "How did it all turn out?"

"It is sure to be a long process of reintegration, but technically, the war is over," Jose says. "A peace treaty has been signed. The guerrillas are currently living in protected areas as they are helped to transition back into Colombian society. They are forming a political party and becoming part of the system. The process is hard because people must forgive and start fresh on both sides."

"I have seen this myself in places like Pine Ridge," I say. "It is easier to remember than it is to forgive. As you look to Colombia's future, what concerns you? Where are the risks?"

"Colombia's biggest challenge is the corruption in its government," Jose replies without hesitation. "Most modern political platforms around the world are corrupt. The corruption I am talking about is different than Mafia corruption, but it's just as powerful, or even more so. Political parties take power, and they hold it by creating lots of jobs and social programs that their communities cannot ultimately afford and may actually not even need. At the end of the day, it's corruption, because it is using resources to buy influence. But many people cannot see this. All the while, the governments of the world just keep getting bigger and bigger, collecting more and more money, taking more and more power and control."

"Power is destined to be more broadly dispersed as more people awaken to the light that dwells within us all," I say. "The enemy of personal power is bureaucratic control. But bureaucracies are clever; they play on our fear of inadequacy. They play on our fear of survival. The bureaucracy says it is here to protect you, and for that message to take hold you must be first convinced that you need protecting.

"You can't go by what organizations say. They all say the right things. You can only go by what they do. An organization either collects power or it disperses it."

"How do you tell power-collecting organizations from power-dispersing ones?" Jose asks.

"You just watch the center," I say. "If the center keeps expanding, then you know you're looking at a power-collecting bureaucracy."

I pause and then ask, "What's the big learning from the messaging campaign that helped close out the civil war?"

"Two things," Jose replies. "First, that you cannot judge others if you want to help people embrace new ideas. The one thing that puts people off is if they think you are being judgmental. Right or wrong does not matter when people feel judged. Second, you must have incontrovertible arguments, like, 'Wouldn't you like to come home for Christmas?'"

"What's next for you?" I ask.

Jose thinks for a moment.

"Deradicalization," Jose replies.

"That's an interesting word," I say. "What does it mean to you?"

"Deradicalization means helping people become aware of their own belief systems," Jose replies. "I think working on this subject has global application and relevance.

"We all adhere to a belief system. Otherwise, we don't have a strategy for dealing with the world. I am interested in communication strategies that can support people as they look inward at their own beliefs. I want to help tribes learn how to question their own narrative. Here in the UK, it is important to help immigrants feel welcome and comfortable, both with where they are from and where they live now. I want to help immigrants realize that no matter where you come from, you will always be from there, but you will also be British. This is your home too. You can be at peace here. You are home."

The dishes have been cleared. All that remain are water, tea, and folded white napkins.

"Take myself, for example," Jose says. "I live here in London now. If I live here for another ten years I will still be one hundred percent Colombian, but I will also be ninety-five percent British. You can be all of who you are right where you are. You can be home anywhere. Being home is a state of mind."

"If everyone could just feel at home, in place, no matter where they are—well, that one idea would change the world," I reply.

* * *

THE REBIRTH OF ORGANIZATIONAL EXCELLENCE is all about reintroducing the conditions of comfort and safety one human at a time. The degree of discomfort can be acute and easy to see at a place like Pine Ridge or in the Middle East. But the discomfort can also be subtle and hard to see—like in a company, where the people who work there feel they have to be careful about how they express themselves.

Shortly after returning from our trip to Kiev and London, I was at our sawmill complex in Bethel, Maine. It was a crisp fall day, and we were having a lunchtime pig roast with the entire crew as part of our quarterly employee huddle. Hancock Lumber had just been selected as one of the Best Places to Work in Maine for the fifth year in a row, and we were honoring everyone on the team for their important role in making that possible. We were celebrating. But we were also digging in, seeking to improve. While the company overall had achieved its highest score ever, the survey results at Bethel had actually gone down.

"Our first priority is to stay focused on the people who work here," I say to the management team as we loosely assemble around a set of plastic tables in the back of the huddle room, near the boilers and turbine that create steam and power for the plant. "We can't get self-absorbed in our own production goals at the expense of the employee experience. Production pressure becomes employee pressure. No one likes to be behind schedule or constantly trying to keep up.

"Hancock Lumber's true value is not defined by revenue growth or profitability. Those are important metrics for our business, but they are outcomes of a higher purpose. The mission of our company is to add real value to the lives of the people who work here. If we get that right, everything else will take care of itself.

"Usually, a CEO shows up at a mill and says, 'Go faster; produce more.' I am here to say just the opposite. Slow down whenever you feel the pace is threatening the employee experience. Just keep putting them first."

Corporations that expand their mission can play a leading role in the transformation of society. Shareholder return should not be the only mission of a great company. In fact, in the new template of the Seventh Power, profit becomes an outcome, not the goal.

When our employee engagement at Hancock Lumber hit record levels, so too did our financial performance. When a company puts a heightened and sincere focus on employees, the employees will double down on the company in return. Help the employees thrive and the company will thrive, almost by default.

A company can become an irresistible place when it broadens its mission. Humanity's biggest challenge is helping every individual on the planet to see their own self-worth and embrace the Seventh Power that dwells within us all. Corporations can become champions of self-worth and accelerators of human enlightenment. But to do something this meaningful, corporations must learn to think bigger. The purpose of a lumber company isn't just to make lumber—it's to advance the lives of the people who work there.

Businesses are uniquely equipped to take on society's biggest challenges, and in the twenty-first century they must rise to the occasion. The church and state bureaucracies that have led for centuries are no longer, unilaterally, going to be able to tackle and solve the planet's largest problems. We are entering a new age of localism in which each business must become an engine of social change.

But for the full potential of industry to be realized, business must learn to think more broadly about its role and potential for creating change. Taking care of the company is essential, but it's no longer enough.

Imagine if every company in the world took on climate change or the creation of a consistent living wage, as their personal responsibility? Suddenly millions of organizations, large and small, are applying their own voice and creativity to move a global needle. But, of course, my favorite opportunity to tackle is human engagement. Work is the place where adults can find their voice, self-actualize, and lead. The Seventh Power is the most capable force on Earth precisely because it includes everyone.

Business must learn to see what the indigenous communities of the world have long known: we are all connected and related. There is no future in the strategy of isolation. If you are a lumber company, making lumber is no longer enough.

Expanding the mission of business is the seventh lesson of the age of shared leadership.

CHAPTER 8

The Elephant in the Room

"Why do you go away? So that you can come back.
So that you can see the place you came from with new
eyes and extra colors.
And the people see you differently too.
Coming back to where you started is not the same as
never leaving."

—TERRY PRATCHETT

Five years after the Holodomor ended, Ringling Bros. and Barnum & Bailey Circus went to Madison Square Garden for twenty-three days. New York was the first stop on the tour, and the circus was so popular that year that it performed twice daily (forty-six shows in all) before caravanning north to Boston. This was America's most famous traveling show, and it would take only one day off before ending the season in Mobile, Alabama, six months later.

For Christmas, our daughter Sydney gave me a framed copy of an original poster from the circus's 1938 Manhattan sojourn. The

216

festive scene features a giant elephant and two clowns in the fore-ground, with the big top and its colorful flags as the backdrop. Few at the time would have guessed that the elephant, the iconic main attraction of "The Greatest Show on Earth," would one day play a leading role in the circus's demise.

In 2016, the Ringling pachyderms marched into retirement in response to activists' protests and public concerns about their treatment. The emotional well-being of a small herd of elephants was taking precedence over the economic needs of an entire indus-try. A sign of the times, indeed.

One year later, on Sunday, May 5, 2017, I traveled from Maine to Providence, Rhode Island, to watch the last-ever performance of the Ringling Bros. Circus extravaganza.

"The elephant that once made the circus helped to end the circus," I said to Alison from our tight row of plastic seats inside the Dunkin' Donuts Center on the evening of the final show.

We had just watched the last act of the famed Ringling Bros. tigers. Their trainer, Taba Maluenda, and his felines received a five-minute standing ovation. Former Ringling Bros. employ-ees from around the world were in the stands to bear witness to the moment. The tigers themselves seemed to know it was over. "Sunday night the lights went out on the Greatest Show on Earth," reported *The Providence Journal* the following day. It was the night the tiger trainer cried.

What's the lesson here? It wasn't the elephant that changed; humanity's sense of right and wrong evolved. An idea that is helpful in one era can be detrimental, or even fatal, in another. The well-being of a small group of elephants had become more import-ant than the circus empire as a whole. Power was being dispersed. The individual was coming first, and the very definition of who qualified as an individual was transcending human form.

Putting individuals second and organizations first may well have helped empires grow for centuries. But today self-centered governance is the leading cause of human engagement malaise and institutional ineffectiveness.

The clock is ticking on this hierarchical dance of old. The playbook of leadership and followership is turning itself inside out. The old model of leadership was about pulling power into the center and putting the needs of the empire first. The new model is about pushing that same power back out and learning to see the individual human spirit as the first priority.

On the way out of the arena I purchased two stuffed elephants as symbolic mascots of the transformation that is unfolding. Like the lesson itself, they were expensive, but priceless.

* * *

A FEW WEEKS LATER I am in the second-floor conference room at Hancock Lumber's Yarmouth store visiting with my friend and HR consultant, Heather Dunbar. Heather is a calm and thoughtful person who specializes in employee engagement and sees the human soul as the most powerful organizational resource on Earth. She is dressed in blue jeans, a white sweater, and a gray infinity scarf. Her face is as fresh as Maine's air, having walked to our meeting from her nearby home.

"How do we bring this new leadership vision of dispersed power down from the mountain?" Heather asks as she pulls a lock of hair behind her right ear.

"We do it by inviting more business owners and executives to reconsider the mission of work," I say. "We should not predetermine the purpose of work without first contemplating the purpose of life. Work should enhance the lives of the people who do it. The

Industrial Revolution assembled human capacity on a large scale to facilitate dramatic growth in the capability of corporations. That was a company-centric time for industry. But this is the twenty-first century, and a new revolution is unfolding with the potential for advancing the human condition to unprecedented heights.

"Everyone understands the economic purposes of work. But I am talking here about something even more valuable: a heightened sense of self-worth. The highest purpose of life is not economic; the same should be true for work. The mission of a modern company should be to enhance the lives of the people who work there by helping each individual self-actualize."

"How does that employee-centric focus align with the traditional corporate objective of profit? Is profit sacrificed?" Heather asks.

"Even if profitability was the core objective, becoming employee centric is the best way to achieve it," I say. "When individuals feel respected, trusted, and heard, they will show great care for their company in return. In this way, the Seventh Power is the new path to organizational excellence. So, ironically, corporate performance improves when the company learns to pivot and first serve the people who work there."

"How do business leaders who want to change their mission and broaden their effectiveness get started?" Heather queries.

"Ultimately, it's all about culture creation," I say. "Culture is something leaders must be super intentional about. The STAR School is one of my favorite examples. That school is good at teaching reading, writing, spelling, and math, but that's not their core mission. The core mission is to help children see their own worth and connectivity to the larger world. So too it must be at Hancock Lumber. At Hancock Lumber, a mill manager's primary responsibility is not just to make lumber. Lots of companies can do that. A mill manager's job is to use the process of making lumber as a platform to enhance the lives of the people doing the work. As society evolves, so too must the meaning of work. The idea of just getting through our workdays so that we can live on the weekends or in retirement is outdated. Work should add spiritual and social value to the lives of the people who do it. Work should be a place that people enjoy and a place where they grow and feel valued. I'm talking about something bigger than just caring for employees. I'm talking about seeing the company as a conduit to help the people find their voice through work."

"I have heard you use the phrase 'putting the work back in its place,'" Heather says. "What does that mean to you?"

"Historically in the lumber industry, a sixty-hour work week was not uncommon," I say. "In addition, pay rates were often low, but because there was so much overtime, the total weekly paycheck came out OK. The whole dynamic was about the individual employee sacrificing for the good of the company. There was a sense that the earlier you arrived, the later you stayed, and the more difficulty you endured, the more loyal and valuable you were to your company. You served, in part, by sacrificing a big piece of your personal energy. Today, with modern manufacturing technology and lean operating systems, work can take less time and consume less human energy. This frees human capacity for broader engagement in the world.

"I mean, we are always going to have to work hard, compete, and be engaged in our jobs, but it no longer needs to be draining or all-consuming.

"At Hancock Lumber, we have used some of our expanding capacity to manufacture and sell more products. But we have also used our productivity growth to just plain work less. Let's make the work more accurate, less stressful, and less time-consuming. That's a value-additive goal for everyone."

"Was that a difficult concept to instill in your company?" Heather asks.

"Yes, at first it was, because it represented a significant shift in thinking," I reply. "Quite a few traditional narratives about business were turned inside out. Initially, it made people cautious.

"We set out to reduce the average hourly work week from forty-eight hours to forty. As often as possible, we try to do this in four ten-hour workdays, creating three nonwork days. To make this happen we had to tackle the traditional overtime pay system, which is outdated and counterproductive. It rewards work taking longer.

"So we took two steps to replace the old pay system. First, we raised our base pay rates pretty significantly. Second, we established a new bonus system we called 'Performance Gold.' This new system paid bonus money for safety, accuracy, efficiency, and productivity growth. It paid for making the work take less time, not more.

"I don't mean to say that this has totally reinvented people's lives. But it's a meaningful start. If people can work just a little bit less while earning a little bit more, that's progress. It's the right direction to be facing."

"In what ways have you asked the leaders at Hancock Lumber to change?" Heather says.

"First, we asked them to accept a new, broader mission. Making lumber and selling building materials is not a big-enough corporate purpose. Sure, we are highly energized by making lumber and supplying construction materials, but the mission is far bigger. The mission is to enhance the lives of the people who work here.

"Second, we invited each manager to supervise others a bit less and work on themselves a bit more. Leadership is about becoming the change. For example, consider something that frustrates you as a manager about how your team does, or does not, perform. Then turn inward and focus on what you have done to create the environment that supports that which frustrates you. Changing other people is hard sledding. Ultimately, we can only change ourselves, and we do so from within. So we are trying to bring an internal focus into our leadership roles.

"Finally, we asked our managers to listen more, and listen differently. The purpose of listening is understanding. The goal is to not judge what people say, but rather to create a safe environment where people will say what they actually think. We want everyone to feel authentically heard. We do not want a single truth or monolithic view of our company to prevail. The truth is a collage of what everyone experiences.

"So in the end we encouraged all our managers to make some pretty big changes. In some ways, we even asked them to just plain do less. We want everyone to lead, and this requires patience for process and dialogue. I must say, our managers have done an exceptional job with this, and it didn't require any real formal training. Leading this way is actually intuitive. Most anyone who sets their mind to it can do it."

"How did people at your company view your travels to places like Pine Ridge and Kiev?" Heather asks.

"At first, people were probably pretty curious and unsure," I say. "But as soon as they saw how it connected back to thinking differently about work, people were quite supportive. Many of my most constructive ideas for work have been found outside of work. This is where that traditional notion of 'staying in your lane' becomes bad advice for the modern age. Increasing management work time from fifty hours a week to sixty does not improve management by twenty percent. In fact, ultimately, it has the opposite effect. Managers need to be leaders. Leaders need to be broadly connected to the planet as a whole. The best ideas for the lumber industry don't just live within sawmills.

"Ultimately, it all comes back to the mission. If the mission is only to make and sell lumber, then it would be odd for me to be supervising anything other than that. But if the company goal is to advance humanity by engaging people in a fresh, empowering way—well, that changes everything. We want our managers—all our employees, for that matter—to have the time and energy to get out of their lane and engage the broader world more deeply in whatever ways it calls to them. The point isn't that everyone should go to Pine Ridge or Kiev. The point is that everyone should make the time to listen to their internal voice and follow it. In an emergency we can double down and go into overtime mode for the company, but that shouldn't be the normative state."

"How were you viewed at places like Pine Ridge and Kiev?" Heather asks.

"Well, that's interesting as well," I say. "For understandable reasons, there is a sentiment within reservation communities that suggests 'only Indians can speak for Indians.' I have personally heard this phrase before, but I was never treated that way. At Pine Ridge, my voice was always respected. Nevertheless, in time I began pressing on this subject and asking my friends there how that philosophy aligned with 'Mitakuye Oyasin' and the wisdom that we are all related. Are the historic, economic, and social challenges at Pine Ridge solely a Lakota issue, purely an indigenous people's issue, or more broadly a human issue? The challenges faced by disenfranchised communities, in my view, are exacerbated by people staying in their lane and not engaging humanity more broadly. If we are all connected, why wouldn't a lumber company executive from Maine interview Holodomor survivors in Kiev and befriend tribal elders like Verola Spider and Catherine Grey Day at Pine Ridge?"

"So the focus at Hancock Lumber has become human engagement," Heather says. "How does a company specifically drive that?"

"I think the key to expanding human engagement is simply to focus on it. When you decide to make everyone's voice important, it's really not that complicated to determine what should follow," I reply. "It's smart business as well. Companies perform better when everyone shares responsibility. When power is dispersed, organizations become more agile, innovative, efficient, and fun. It all comes down to trusting the talents of others. A company where everyone is expected and encouraged to lead will outperform companies where the decision-making responsibility is held in the hands of a few. The world is flat today, and every person in a company needs to constantly make fast, independent decisions. Hierarchies were built for a slower, older time when we could all wait in line for an audience before the throne."

"You make this sound quite simple," Heather says. "But if the path is that easy to follow, why aren't more companies doing it?"

"The biggest enemy of creating a fresh work culture is the lack of time spent working on it," I reply. "Employee engagement should be the top priority for senior leaders. It should be the one initiative CEOs don't delegate. Leaders also need to go back to the beginning and revisit the very premise and purpose of work itself. We need to set a bigger goal. Business can advance humanity. When this happens, profit becomes an outcome of a higher calling."

"What's your core advice for established leaders?" Heather asks, leaning back in her chair.

"First, I would say it's for leaders to learn to stop worrying about everyone else so much. We are each here to bring the best version of ourselves forward. It's the understanding that me working on me yields the greatest rewards.

"Second, I would say it's learning to see the business as more than just an economic engine. Of course, profitability is important. A company cannot sustain itself without profitability—but that is more of an outcome than a goal. The goal of a great company should be to improve the lives of the people who work there."

* * *

DISPERSING POWER IS NOT HARD TO DO. It's about learning how to defer to the most fundamental laws of nature. But creating a culture where every voice matters does require discipline and intentionality. Humanity's modern thirst for deep change is real, but to get there, the established organizational rules must be thoughtfully deconstructed. At Hancock Lumber, deepening employee engagement is our number-one goal. We believe that if we get that right, everything else we care about will materialize.

At the core of our engagement system is the annual Best Places to Work in Maine survey. Every year all our employees go online and complete a questionnaire in which they are asked to describe their workplace as they experience it. Every answer is confidential, and no individual is ever connected to a specific response.

Here are just a few examples of the eighty work experience topics that our team members are asked to consider and evaluate:

- *"The leaders of this organization are open to input from employees."*
- *"I feel I can express my honest opinion without fear of negative consequences."*
- *"I am given enough authority to make the decisions I need to make."*
- *"My supervisor helps me develop to my fullest potential."*
- *"My pay is fair for the work I perform."*

- *"My job provides me with a sense of meaning and purpose."*
- *"Senior leaders live the core values of this organization."*
- *"A spirit of trust and cooperation exists at work."*

These are great prompts for conversation and inquiry as they get to the essence of a company's culture and work environment. At Hancock Lumber, we have chosen to make this survey the paramount measurement of how we are doing as a company. It's the voice of the employees made strong, and the annual engagement score that results is our most anticipated metric (more so even than our financial results). The survey is the annual kickoff to what we have designed to be a five-step engagement-enhancement process.

Step 1: Survey

The survey is completed, typically with 95 percent participation from our 525 employee associates.

Step 2: Analyze

The survey responses are sorted for us by mill, store, and age group. We then take that data and plot the trends from previous years to see which categories of engagement are gaining strength and which ones might be slipping.

The data speaks for itself: Is engagement statistically strengthening? Where are the cracks and vulnerabilities in our work experience as defined by the people who work here? Are certain questions or themes scoring low? Where are the most important opportunities to improve? What are strong points to be celebrated? These are the questions that define Step 2 as we analyze the data and look for the patterns.

Step 3: Huddles

Each store and mill, at a local level, then identify a self-selected set of survey topics for deeper employee inquiry. These are subjects that typically have lower scores, but we also select those with fast-rising scores. Here is an example of a theme that scored lower than we would like in our most recent survey:

- *"Changes that affect me are communicated prior to implementation."*

Once a target issue has been identified, we enter into small huddle groups where six to ten employees at a location sit around a table with a few representatives from company management. The object now is to share the selected topic with the focus group in order to get deeper clarification and feedback: Does it surprise you that this subject scored lower this year than last? Why do you feel the score went down? If you alone were responsible, what might you do to improve people's experience and perception in this area? These are the types of questions that we ask in focus group.

During this stage of the process it is critical not to judge or negatively respond to the perspectives the group shares. Initially, the mission of the huddle is not to change or fix anything; we are simply seeking to understand. No perspectives are refuted or rebutted in these circles. Every voice is respected. It's the world as our employees currently experience it. Like the Navajo peacemakers, the goal is to allow everyone to feel heard.

One of the last acts of Step 3 is to ask the huddle participants what they would suggest doing in order to make improvements in the areas we are exploring. I call this moment the "answers to the test." What we have found time and again is that people are smart, and they care. They know what would improve almost any situation they experience; they have the answers and will lead the implementation if invited to do so. All leadership has to do is ask the right questions and then follow through.

Step 4: Initiatives

Step 4 is where the follow-through happens. Here, we launch initiatives. Typically, they are simple, inexpensive, and easy-to-deploy action steps. We look first for the small ways the experience can be quickly improved. For the most part, it's just doing what the focus group teams have already suggested. These initiatives come out of the gate with strong buy-in because we are simply taking the answers that were given to us and implementing them.

Step 5: More Huddles/Feedback

A few weeks (or months) later, we go back to the huddle groups and ask if they've noticed any positive changes as a result of the initiatives that have been set in motion. This leads to more feedback, either affirming that we're on the right path or making it clear that some additional (or new) approach is still necessary.

By the time this five-step process has run its course, a year has passed, and we are eager to take another survey and collect fresh data once again. It's an iterative cycle that never expires—lean management principles applied to employee engagement—and absolutely the most important work we do at Hancock Lumber. Getting the culture right in the eyes of our employee associates is the number-one priority for managers and supervisors (especially the CEO).

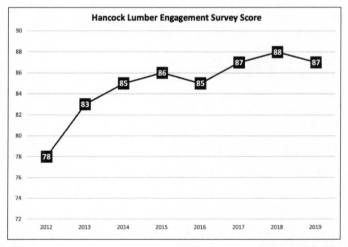

This is our company's overall survey score through 2019. Close to ninety percent of our team confidentially describes themselves as highly engaged in their work and in the mission of the organization. According to Gallup, the national average for this figure hovers between 30 and 35 percent. Most people are not inspired by their work. What a shame.

Recently, I was standing in our planing mill in Bethel as boards were streaming through the molder to be patterned and then packaged for their final destination. I was saying hi to one of the supervisors in the area when I noticed a legal pad under the metal conveyor chain at his side. The pages were a bit worn and full of handwritten notes. On top of the pad was the simple heading "Ideas for Strengthening Engagement."

"What's this?" I ask, peering down through my safety glasses.

"Oh, it's just the list of questions I want to ask the guys at our next huddle," the supervisor says.

I put my hand on his shoulder and smile, ready to hug him right then and there in the middle of the shift.

"That's awesome!" I reply. "I love this! It's exactly what I'm hoping every supervisor in our company will do. Great job! This makes my day. Thank you."

As we shake hands, I can see the pride in his eyes.

The questions, handwritten on that yellow note pad, were more valuable than the boards traveling above it:

"What wastes your time?"

"What changes might you make to improve the production flow and work experience?"

"How might communication be improved? What would you like to know more about?"

"What do you enjoy most about your work? What do you like least?"

It's not the questions that are complicated. It's creating the right environment where the questions are asked at all and then answered honestly. It is essential that it's safe to speak the truth, otherwise people often won't.

Under the right conditions leadership gets easy because the work of leading is shared by everyone. Employees who work on the front line of a business know best what problems exist and what the solutions might be. All management has to do is create a safe environment—ask the right questions—listen without judgment—confirm understanding—and then follow up and implement the changes.

"Are staffing levels adequate?" This is a question in our most recent survey that scored lower than we would like. So we go into employee huddles and ask people to tell us more about their views on that subject. The conversation might go something like this:

Manager: "Does it surprise you that this question scored low?"

Employee: "No, it doesn't surprise me."

Manager: "Can you tell me more about why it doesn't surprise you?"

Employee: "Yes, I can. Every morning from seven to ten, when the store and yard are filled with contractors picking up their supplies for the day, we aren't able to help everyone get loaded."

Manager: "Thanks for sharing that. Are there other times of the day or week when perhaps we might have more people than we need? Could we shift some resources in the schedule?"

Employee: "Yes. Typically, after three p.m. it gets pretty quiet in the yard. We could cover things with one fewer person in the afternoon."

Manager: "That seems easy enough to try. I will shift some work hours forward from the end of the day to the beginning. Does that make sense?"

Employee: "That does makes sense."

Manager: "What else might help this issue?"

Employee: "Well, many of our vendor deliveries arrive from seven to ten a.m. as well. If we could get some of our vendors to deliver in the afternoon, that would be beneficial."

Manager: "Thanks for sharing that. I will talk to Purchasing and see if we can make that happen. Next week, at huddle, I'll update you."

When the culture is safe, the improvement discussions become very simple.

My number-one wish for any organization is that it is a safe place for everyone to say what they think. Differing perspectives don't need to be hushed or refuted. When everyone is heard, magic unfolds and work becomes something more than just an economic exercise. It's a simple formula that any leader can follow, but it does require restraint and a new philosophy about listening. What you do as a leader when someone offers a view that is different than your own is pivotal. The culture of the company is ultimately defined by the way leaders respond to ideas that don't match their own view of the world.

Perhaps leaders have traditionally resisted this approach because they fear they will lose control. But what we have seen at Hancock Lumber is that just the opposite occurs. When everyone is invited to participate in decision-making, the support for those decisions grows. People will own what they help create.

* * *

I ONCE ATTENDED A BROADWAY PLAY in which some of the seats, including mine, were actually on the stage—an awkward feeling at first, to be sure. As the show rolled along an actor or actress would occasionally pause at our table, and one even sat in my lap. At that moment I was both inside and outside the show.

Writing this book has a similar feel to me. I believe there is an energy field that binds all that was, is, and shall be. What is learned by one is value-added to another. None of my learning is original. It came from, and belongs to, us all.

On the day Evan and I went for ice cream it had been seven years since I'd acquired spasmodic dysphonia, at the peak of the national housing and mortgage market collapse. And it had been six years since I'd begun traveling to the Pine Ridge Indian Reservation. The two events combined to help me realize that there are lots of ways to lose your voice in this world. It's common to not feel fully heard.

In time I came to see my voice disorder as an invitation to live and lead differently. Leaders, I now realized, had often done more to restrict the voices of others than to liberate them. Leaders, overtly or otherwise, were often holding back humanity from progressing at its optimal pace. The needs of the organization were taking precedence over the needs of the individuals. This was the script that needed to be flipped. Power, long collected by the capitals of organizations, was destined to be dispersed and shared.

I decided a while ago that I wanted to be a small part of making that change occur. So I first set out to change myself from within. To do that, I needed to get out of the confines of my narrow lane. A year of periodic travel and experiential learning followed.

The leaders of the STAR School showed me the Navajo values of peacemaking and the importance of culture creation. Great people are everywhere. Culture makes the difference.

In Nashville I joined a community united through spasmodic dysphonia that was refusing to give up the search for their own true voice. There I saw the potential of accepting each voice as it is. I also realized that listening was actually the path to progressive leadership.

In the backcountry of Wind Cave National Park, I celebrated the regenerative benefits of spending time alone in wild places.

Wind Cave is a place where I can turn inward and swap ego for self-awareness. Alone in the wilderness, I have no titles, no roles, and no accomplishments. Here, I feel my connection to all that exists in the Universe.

In Boston, in the shadows of the great cathedral at Copley Square, I pedaled, cried, and felt reborn on a yellow bike that went nowhere. Here I saw an example of making individual well-being the organizational goal. SoulCycle was flipping the script on the traditional business model where the organization came first. In this way, SoulCycle was making the headquarters smaller. Modern organizations can thrive by putting individuals first.

Back home in Maine, at the Seeds of Peace Camp, I learned that we all have about half the story right. There I met the Paradigm Shifters and experienced firsthand a social model for the new age that was turning teenagers into global peacemakers. It was this remote camp that helped confirm for me that change is an inside job. We must all learn to listen, first to ourselves and then to others, without judgment. Understanding is the objective of listening.

Next, Alison and I were off to Kiev, where a sobering story of genocide provided inspirational testimony to the resilience of the human spirit. Mykola and Hanna each shared their voices with such grace that it felt surreal to be in their presence. On this trip I experienced the value of getting out of my lane and taking advantage of the flatness of the modern world. Lumber alone would not define me.

At ZEO we engaged with a group of inspiring young leaders working to create a "new normal" for society. In London, Jose Miguel Sokoloff shared the story of how Christmas trees and soccer balls transcended fifty years of bloodshed, division, and war. Jose also described his vision of how everyone might someday feel at home, right where they are. Both encounters reinforced the transformative value of broadening the mission of a company to include all of humanity.

When I reflected on the entire journey, seven lessons crystallized:

#1 GREAT PEOPLE are everywhere.
#2 CULTURE makes the difference.
#3 CHANGE is created first from within.
#4 LOCALIZE and shrink the center.
#5 LISTEN for understanding, not judgment.
#6 OVERREACHING has consequences.
#7 BROADEN the mission.

I have come to think of them collectively as the Seven Lessons of the Age of Shared Leadership. These seven learnings form a circle of growth that can propel any organization. Social change can become the first business of business, but it must be engineered one soul at a time.

Ultimately, every leader has the choice to either collect authority or disperse it. Every follower has the choice to either live someone else's truth or find their own. Each organization has the choice to either create a culture that extends the drag of the mega-bureaucracies or accelerate the arrival of the new social order of shared leadership. In the end, it's all personal. Consciously or otherwise, we each make one choice or the other.

As Joseph Campbell said, "We are the truth we seek to know." To improve the world, I need only look inward. To change the world, I must first change myself. The ultimate choice that belongs equally to all of us is the orientation we select. I can work on me, or I can wait for you. To realize that we are each the star of our own stories is liberating.

I am the one who needs to change.

I am the one who needs to grow.

I am the one and only version of me that this world will ever see, and I should do whatever I can to bring the best me forth.

I belong to the human symphony, and I have one responsibility: to bring forth my authentic voice.

The Sioux and the Navajo knew all this ages ago. This is long-held knowledge. Each of us is unique by design, sacred by nature, and connected to all that is and shall be. We are each *Wakan Yeja*. We are each the Seventh Power.

* * *

It's a fall Saturday afternoon and I am sitting in my office holding one of the cuddly, stuffed pachyderms from the circus in my lap as I type.

His dark blue eyes stare up at me as if he is somehow alive, which causes me to do a double take. Meanwhile, across the room I can hear one of my favorite songs, "Scare Away the Dark" by Passenger, playing on the black Sonos speaker below the television, paying homage to the power of the light that dwells within us all.

Humanity is capable of creating great darkness, fueled by fear, greed, and the absence of self-awareness. I have seen the vestiges of this firsthand at Pine Ridge, the Navajo Nation, Seeds of Peace, and in Kiev. But I have also seen, in each of those places, a great light.

During my year of travel and contemplation, I concluded that culture is the organizational differentiator on Planet Earth. It has long been held that people make the difference, but great people are everywhere. The planet is full of them and always has been. Certain cultures create conditions where people can thrive—where they are free to be their authentic selves—while others discourage self-expression. Certain cultures celebrate the Seventh Power, while others attempt to thwart it, both intentionally and otherwise.

In the end the differences between a constructive and a destructive culture are simple. Is the bureaucratic center of the tribe always seeking to grow bigger and gain more power? Or is the center dispersing itself and reveling in a tactical supporting role? Does the community speak with one monolithic, centralized voice? Or is this a place where every voice is honored in a symphony of shared leadership? Are people shunned when they have differing perspectives, or are they thanked and praised? Is the creativity and agility of localized action revered or discouraged? At the Seeds of Peace Camp there are finger snaps of approval when someone speaks with their own true voice, regardless of whether you happen to share that particular view. It's one of those rare places where agreement is not necessary for solidarity.

Human epochs have defining cultural characteristics. Like the Ringling Bros. elephants, what was helpful in one age can be harmful in another. This poses challenges equally shared among those who think they lead and those who feel they are following.

In the new age of the Seventh Power, a fresh set of cultural paradigms is unfolding. How messy this transition becomes and how long it takes to play out are really up to all of us, but those who hold formal positions of leadership have an extra layer of opportunity and responsibility.

In the decades to come many long-standing organizational norms will invert themselves. This will be a big change, not a small one. Increasingly, leaders are going to gain influence by making themselves smaller, not bigger. Decision-making responsibility is going to be shared, not collected. And most importantly, the truth is going to become fluid, not rigid. While this will feel scary to many at first, the scales will eventually tip. This is because it is

actually liberating and energizing on all sides to foster and cultivate a community where everybody leads.

I do believe that the cure for the planet's human engagement
slump lives within us all. It's called the Seventh Power, and in the
bureaucratic halls of the world's past-based institutions, it is the
elephant in the room.

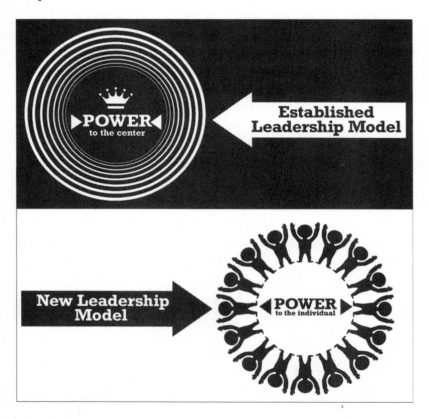

The Path to Healing

"The wound is the place where the Light enters you."

—RUMI

A t every stop this book chronicles, I found people searching for their voice. And I was one of them.

When you are diagnosed with SD, you are told immediately that your condition is incurable. But this established medical "truth" has never fully resonated with me. Many people who acquire the disorder do so during a highly tumultuous period in their life when something dear hangs in the balance. Thus was the case for me. My voice condition arrived as a consequence of the stress I had unknowingly internalized in the years surrounding the housing market collapse. At the time I couldn't distinguish my individual identity from the role I played as CEO. A wound to the business was a wound to me. In those days, especially under duress, I led with a superstrong voice. In times of trouble, I frequently became dogmatic, impulsive, and overpowering.

But then SD arrived. It was a loving gift in disguise. It was an invitation to live differently, lead differently, and self-actualize.

And, in time, I changed.

So why couldn't the vocal condition recede once the lessons it came to impart had been learned? If one set of internal conditions brought it on, why couldn't a new state of spiritual and emotional awareness set it free?

Early in 2018, my attention to my voice heightened when the Botox injections I systematically received stopped working. Until that time I had been lazy and externally focused with respect to my own rehabilitation. When my voice got bad, I drove to Boston, sat in a procedure chair for five minutes, and got a shot. Someone else, out there, owned the responsibility for improving my situation.

Suddenly, my ability to depend upon an external source for my internal relief was gone. If I was going to improve, it would now have to come from within.

So what did I do?

Well, first I forgot everything I had learned since 2010, and I panicked!

I spent most of 2018 making all the same mistakes SD had come to help my soul transcend. I fought my voice. I put curing it on a timetable. I pushed, worried, complained, and got angry (like that was going to help). I thrashed about like a fish in a rowboat.

Of course, SD was going nowhere with me in that frenzied state of being. I think my spirit guides must have sighed and shaken their heads. *What a problem case I'd turned out to be*, they must have thought. *Will this dude ever learn?*

But later in the year, with the help of some very talented and loving facilitators—a wife, a healer, a massage therapist, a mindfulness coach, a hypnotherapist, and a speech therapist—I began to truly calm myself, listen, and go to work. For the first time since onset, I started to closely study my voice from the inside out.

As I began to focus on the nuances of my voice, I noticed that it was actually very inconsistent and that my speech struggles were often conditional. I didn't always have a strained and choppy voice; in fact, I frequently had short moments of normalcy. This was frustrating but encouraging. On the edges of my mostly weak voice, a healthy voice still lived. How fascinating!

Every morning, when I woke up, for example, I started the day with a defect-free voice. Sleep unwound the broken speaking patterns. My true voice might only last for an hour or so, but sure enough, it was still there within me. Additionally, when I talked to myself, my voice tended to mostly normalize. After years of self-reflection, hallmarked by my travels to Pine Ridge, my voice constrictions had evolved and become conditional.

"I only have trouble talking to other humans," I was now fond of saying.

In my revitalized quest for a vocal recovery, I learned a lot about the human brain. The big realization was that my brain (and yours) is actually quite pliable. The brain has patterns, but those patterns can be changed. Within this knowledge is the narrow, winding path to a cure.

As I paid closer and closer attention to my voice, the patterns and lessons that began to surface struck me as universally human learnings. First, I had to let go of my external dependence on Botox. Next, I had to start looking internally for solutions and realize that I held within me the power to effectuate change. Finally, any progress I made would need to begin with baby steps. There was no express lane to the cure I sought. If I wanted to get better, I was going to have to learn to crawl first.

So I began revisiting the way I breathed, swallowed, and pro-
cessed air.

"Don't believe your symptoms cannot be cured," my friend
Karen Higley reminded me one day, as we visited at her home.
Karen is a massage therapist and a spiritualist, attuned to that
which we can and cannot see.

"Put your consciousness in your throat and just fill it up
with love. Invite your spirit guides to put their love there too,"
Karen said.

* * *

ONE WEEK LATER, I WAS SITTING DOWNSTAIRS at Pat's Pizza on
Route 1 in Yarmouth, Maine, with a friend, talking about the possibility that we all incarnate with the intention to outgrow certain
karmic patterns that have traveled with us from a past lifetime.
Life—souls included—wants to evolve.

"I'm sorry to interrupt," the woman at the next table said. "I
heard a bit of your discussion and feel compelled to tell you that I
just had the most amazing experience with a medium from Portland. Her name is Sarah Winslow."

I was quite proud that someone from a neighboring table could
hear me.

Two weeks later, I was sitting with Sarah Winslow in her small
third-floor office on St. John Street in Portland.

"This room is full of spirits that are here to help you," Sarah
said. "They want you to remember that your condition can be
cured. Don't be fooled, they keep telling me; don't be fooled. Your
condition *can* be cured. But they want you to know that it can only
be cured from within.

"You need to see Chloe Urban," Sarah said, her eyes closed. "She is a healer. She can help you."

Chloe Urban. I repeated the name in my head with the same care I took one year ago for the phrase *In nature, power is dispersed.*

Two weeks later I was lying down in Chloe's office as she performed a set of exercises to determine the underlying nature of my affliction. Chloe uses a combination of shamanic practices, neuroscience, soulful counseling, heightened sensitivity to energy waves, and pure love to activate her client's internal capacity to heal their own wounds.

"Your body is designed to be perfectly healthy," Chloe said. "Your spirit is an infinite being; it knows everything necessary for you to cure yourself from within. First, however, we must become conscious about the origins of your disease. Is it physical, mental, spiritual, emotional, or genetic? Is the wound trauma based? Is the wound even your energy at all, or did it come from another? Is the wound from this lifetime, or is it reflective of a past-life experience? Once we gain consciousness regarding the root causes, we can hopefully release them."

The session that followed felt transformational. At the end, as we sat together on the couch, I spoke effortlessly in my normal voice. While I sensed that this moment might be difficult to sustain, it demonstrated yet again that my authentic voice still lived within me.

"Tomorrow I want you to take a hot bath," Chloe instructed. "Squeeze the juice from four lemons into the water and add two cups of Epsom salts. Stay in there for at least thirty minutes. This will help any remaining energy that does not belong to you to clear itself."

"OK," I replied, fully committed.

On Saturday I ran out to the local store and bought eight lemons and two bags of Epsom salts. The clerk looked at me quizzically, but I didn't flinch. Both Saturday and Sunday I filled the tub, squeezed in the lemon juice, and poured in the salts. The scene made me laugh.

"Vampires," I said sarcastically.

In the two weeks that followed my voice was all over the charts. I had moments, mostly alone, when my voice was free of SD symptoms. But then I had other periods where my voice was highly constricted. I didn't know why the extreme fluctuations were occurring.

On the day of the spring equinox I returned to Chloe's office for a second session.

"I would definitely take that up-and-down performance of your voice as an encouraging signal," Chloe said. "Your voice wound is deep and has been in place for a long time. Healing will be a process. Today we'll see if we can do more sourcing of the remaining energy that still wants to be released."

Chloe takes me back in time, stopping at the age of five, where she senses the origins of some of the restrictive energy.

"Was there something about your mother or father and your relationship to feeling loved that might have triggered discomfort within you at that time?" Chloe asked. "This wound could be conscious or unconscious, so you may or may not recall. Think about how you interpreted being loved."

Something about that invitation triggered an understanding within me.

"There is no specific event that comes to mind," I said, "but this was a time in my relationship with my dad when perhaps I began to feel the need to perform in a certain way that I thought pleased him. This was when school started, and it was about getting the right grades and playing sports the right way. It was about dressing a certain way, shaking hands a certain way, behaving a certain way.

"So yes, that could have been internalized: to feel that love needed to be earned. With my mom it felt different—unconditional. But even then I felt my mom also had to act a certain way to receive the reinforcement that I would have identified as loving. There is no animosity or sadness in this reflection. Today, I know my dad's love is unconditional, but I think he was living out some wounds of his own at that time, like we all do."

A tear rolled down my right cheek as I looked up at Chloe.

"That's a piece of the energy we are seeking to release," Chloe said. "Any energy that feels it must perform or accomplish to be loved is represented by constriction in your voice and the events that triggered it. The new energy you want to take in is unconditional love.

"Your being was transformed during this process of traveling to Pine Ridge and searching for your voice," Chloe continued. "Occasionally, someone who has a near-death experience, like from a car accident, will recall the departure of one being and the entry of another. But you did this on your own, without a physical accident. It was a transformation of being, and that altered how you feel on the inside and how you see and relate to the world around you."

"I do feel reborn in terms of how I experience both myself and the world," I replied, as another tear ran down my cheek. "I know that a transformation occurred. I just haven't had the context to define it."

"Your voice constriction is a manifestation of your old being, with an old wound," Chloe said. "Totally clearing that energy is not something that happens quickly, or easily. Between now and our next session I want you to do some inquiry around this. I want you to write about it. But I want you to do so without any negative energy or judgment. You should have nothing but love for your earlier being."

Later that night, I was sitting in my office at home. The oil lantern on my desk burned as I read the list of questions Chloe had asked me.

"What are the qualities of your new being?"

It's calm—unidentified by roles—feels light and relaxed—it's not worried about outcomes—it's not put off by the perspectives of others—it's collaborative—it sees the connectivity—it's in the moment—it trusts the future—it worries less—it judges less—it loves everything where it is. It sees humanity as a small family— enjoys its responsibilities but is not consumed by them—it's curious—it seeks to learn, but is comfortable with the process of not knowing—it smiles—it's unbridled, and wants to laugh at the magnificence of being.

"What qualities are unique to the old being? What are you letting go of?"

I am letting go of anxiety—fear of performing. I am letting go of seeing my identity as the results of my work. I am letting go of proving my worth through accomplishments. But this hasn't made me less interested in my roles; on the contrary, it has liberated me from them so that I can pursue them with less fear and more joy. I'm letting go of trying to be the savior—the protector. I am letting go of having to be right. I am letting go of dogma and using my position or the tone of my voice to intimidate others when I feel threatened. I am letting go of winning and losing. I am letting go of validation through achievements. I am letting go of ego. I am letting go of doing what I think others expect I should do. In my new being I can actually see myself. I can see my shortcomings and mistakes, but they don't make me judgmental. I am letting go of judgment. I don't feel any animosity toward any past wounds or pieces of who I am. Every part of me has brought me to this moment. It's all valuable and all to be loved.

＊ ＊ ＊

SEVERAL MONTHS LATER, at Chloe's suggestion, I found myself at the Angels' Rest Retreat Center in the western mountains of Massachusetts for a three-day program of the Infinity Healing School led by Gabrielli LaChiara.

In 2003, Gabrielli was diagnosed with advanced breast cancer and was told that she might not survive. "I could feel the life spirit leaving me," she would later confide. "I knew at that moment that I needed to completely change my orientation if I was going to survive."

Not only did Gabrielli survive, she thrived, and fifteen years later she leads this well-regarded school of self-healing. This was the last day of the program, and all thirty-six participants were moving quietly across the great hall where we had assembled all weekend.

"Certain spots in this room will have more meaning for you than others," Gabrielli said. "Feel those spots and celebrate the memory of what occurred there."

I was happy with the weekend. I felt calm, peaceful, and centered. But I did not feel cured. My voice had been good at times, not good at others. Part of me had hoped that a miracle would occur and that I would leave with a "normal" voice. That had not happened. Nonetheless, it had been a meaningful experience, and I was leaving with a warm heart and some new skills.

Suddenly, it hit me.

This is my voice. It's not broken. This is my voice.

That simple message came seemingly out of nowhere. I remember actually hearing it whispered to me externally before I repeated and internalized what I had heard. I was standing near the corner of the large area rug by the picture window overlooking the forest, in the exact spot where Melissa, Ruth, and I had "journeyed" for each other yesterday. (Journeying is the act of holding energy and pure love for another for an extended period, with no judgment or responsibility toward healing that person in any way.)

This is my voice. It's not broken. This is my voice.

These three sentences were triggered by a question Gabrielli had posed: "Where would you be without your disease?" Standing in silence on that carpet, the entire world around me melted away. In a room full of people, I felt as if I was the only person there.

Where would I be without SD?

The answer for me was joyously clear: I would be much worse off. I hadn't lost my voice; I had found it. SD had not taken anything away. It had brought me home.

With this new realization I whispered the chant Gabrielli had taught us: "I invoke, incant, proclaim, and pronounce that I no longer have SD."

I repeated this statement softly, but with conviction, nine times.

Before the tenth recital I paused to locate Chloe. I walked toward her, grabbing both of her arms upon arrival. "I invoke, incant, proclaim, and pronounce that I no longer have SD," I said.

Chloe instantly understood what had transpired. Healing, for me, had just been redefined.

While I had been hoping for a sudden and miraculous physical transformation, this was not the healing that was coming my way. Healing meant something different. Healing was the act of self-acceptance. It was about owning my voice as it is, and not fighting it or considering it to be foreign or wounded. My unique and never-to-be-repeated voice is a gift, just like yours.

I made a choice at that moment: never again would I say that I have SD. For the first time since onset, I accepted my post-2010 voice as my own.

Jose Sokoloff has a wish for all the peoples of the world—to feel at home, at peace, and in place, exactly where and as they are. While I had been championing this understanding at Hancock Lumber and throughout the process of writing this book, it was only in this moment that I finally claimed it for myself.

It reminded me of something my dear friend Catherine Grey Day had said to me at Pine Ridge exactly one month earlier. At the time I had been confused by her guidance, but suddenly her message became clear. The two of us were sitting at the weathered picnic table under the porch at the Singing Horse Trading Post while she skimmed the manuscript that would become this book.

"Kevin, you have become a relative to me," Catherine said. "So listen to what I have to say, as I am your older sister: You may no longer have your original physical voice, but it brought you something more powerful. This is your voice—and it's stronger now than it was before. Your voice is a gift. You just need to learn to own it."

One tear and then another rolled down her cheeks beneath her dark glasses.

"You speak of your voice as a disorder, but you've gotta quit that negative thinking. It's not a disorder; it's *your voice*. You just need to love yourself as you are, and then, in time, you can have your own speaking voice back."

* * *

SHORTLY AFTER THE RETREAT AT ANGELS' REST, I decided to truly double down and make my voice my first priority. Within weeks I was working with a speech therapist, a hypnotherapist, and a mindfulness coach. I was also doing daily breathing and vocal exercises, drinking lots of water, and carefully contemplating the internal neurological patterns that triggered my voice.

As the year drew to a close, I even spent ten days alone on a self-guided voice retreat. By this point I had tried everything but rest to restore my voice. The entire experience felt generative and caring. I was putting me first—something I had been encouraging others to do for years but had yet to fully embrace for myself.

During one of many soulful sessions with my hypnotherapist, Maggie Clement, I realized for the first time that the vocal tightening I experienced no longer originated in my throat. The seizing of my chest preceded and initiated the squeezing of my throat. I'm not sure this was always the case, but it was my situation now. After eight years of searching I had located the physical origins of my problem. I was excited! I've always felt that awareness, in and of itself, is powerful and leads to change.

Maggie's sessions would become a cornerstone of my personal voice recovery protocol. The word, 'hypnosis,' is widely misunderstood. The process, in essence, has two simple steps. It begins with a period of relaxation similar to meditation, followed by a series of visualizations. In my case, I visualize conversations in a variety of settings in which my voice is performing as if I never acquired SD. During these visualizations I talk and talk with ease. I say everything I want to say and each word is clear and effortless. Everyone hears what I say with ease. There is no tension in my voice. It's fun to talk and I keep going, telling stories and carrying on.

"The brain does not distinguish between these visualizations and a real event," Maggie explained. "To the brain, visualizations during hypnosis are real events. During those sessions, the patterns of effortless speech are re-established."

Maggie would go on to teach me self-hypnosis and it is now part of my daily morning routine. Before leaving the house each morning, I sit in a comfortable chair in my study, light a candle in front of my most sacred Pine Ridge collectibles, and then relax and visualize. In this way, every day, I experience a fully-functional voice with which the simple act of speaking becomes enjoyable and exciting once more!

The understanding that the brain is pliable is exceptionally powerful. The human brain can acquire unwanted patterns but so too, therefore, can it acquire desired ones. As science and spirituality learn to tap deeper into this amazing truth, the potential for growth and healing is without boundary. We can create discomfort within ourselves and we can also achieve and restore optimal health, balance, and joy. We really are exceptional creatures that still have so much to learn about the capacities that dwell within us all—long known to the Sioux as the Seventh Power.

A month later, during a session with Chloe, my self-awareness was heightened yet again. Chloe was guiding me through a "clearing" session, designed to identify and then release any energy sources within my body that were neither mine nor helpful to my healing. I found this one of the most interesting parts of Chloe's practice. When you feel tension, worry, or disease, you must learn to ask yourself: What is the origin of that energy? Does it even belong to me? Does that energy serve me? If the answer to the last question is no, then you learn to release that energy away from your body and gift it back to the Light of Consciousness.

Chloe paused with her hands over my chest and asked me to focus on the origins of the tension she had identified there, initiated during speech.

"What is the source of this energy?" Chloe asked.

Some time passed. My eyes were closed, my breathing, deep and rhythmic. And then the answer came to me.

"I gave it to myself," I said. "It's a gift from my own soul. The voice condition was a guide to help put me on my true path in this lifetime. I knew I was going to need a push to make the change I wanted to create. SD was that push, and I put it there."

"Yes," Chloe said, as if she'd known the answer all along. "And if it were to leave now, would you be able to stay on your path? Are you ready for it to go?"

There was a pause.

"Yes," I replied. "I am ready for it to go."

"OK, then let's release and surrender that energy back to the Light of Consciousness," Chloe said with a smile.

"Let's do that," I said, smiling in return.

＊ ＊ ＊

THE FIRST STEP TO FINDING YOUR VOICE IS LOSING IT. The second step is taking up the search. I know this because I have walked that path.

Humanity's shared quest to release our authentic voice is the real mission of a life on Earth. Leaders in the twenty-first century can make a transformational contribution to human evolution by supporting, not thwarting, this inextinguishable search. Strengthening the voice is something all of us are called to do.

Dynamic leadership in the new age of the Seventh Power is about helping others to self-actualize. In this model, the organization becomes a service platform for individual self-exploration and growth. Where are the places where adults can continue to grow? The workplace is the prime candidate. It takes great skill and care for a team of people to be successful. Companies must learn to carefully cultivate the cultural conditions of human success in the twenty-first century. But for any of this to occur, the leaders themselves must become the first to change.

There is no end point to the process of self-actualization. There is no finish line; there is just a continuum. Each learning opens a new door into a strange room where more growth is invited to occur. Wherever you are on that journey is exactly where you are supposed to be. Open each new door in peace, with the gift of knowing that you're already home. You and your voice are amazing right now, exactly as you are.

✳ ✳ ✳

IN THE CLASSIC FAIRY TALE OR DISNEY STORY, something magical always happens in the end. But in the human experience, the path to magic lives in the love of the ordinary.

After years of traveling to Pine Ridge—and then around the globe on the adventures contained in this book—I now find myself learning to breathe by blowing bubbles.

That's right, bubbles.

Three times a day, I sit with a small plastic cup and a straw. The bottom third of the cup is filled with water. I blow bubbles into the cup and then hum through the straw while still blowing bubbles. With practice, I have learned to transition continuously from bubbles without noise to bubbles with noise. Back and forth I go. Bubbles without noise…bubbles with noise…bubbles without noise. The entire time, my airway is open. You can't blow bubbles without air.

When I do this at home, I light the evergreen candle in my office where all my artifacts from Pine Ridge sit in a sort of personal shrine. I say a brief prayer to the Great Spirit, Wakan Tanka, and surrender to the Light of Consciousness.

Then I go to work.

The noise I make is reminiscent of the sacred Hindu Aum chant, which signifies the essence of primordial sound and true consciousness. The process gives me confidence. After weeks of practice I know that I can make a sound and keep my airway open. The muscles in my lower abdomen are actually sore when I finish—that's how long I have gone without fully opening my airway while speaking. There are muscles down there to support speech that have gone unused for years.

A week later I take a big step. While making noise and bubbles in the cup, I pull the straw out of the water and make the Aum sound through the straw into the open air. Now I can make a clear noise without the water.

The next week, I do the same, but this time I slowly pull the straw away from my mouth. Now I can make a clear noise without the water or the straw. I can actually picture that airway forming a clear and unobstructed circle through which air continuously flows.

Personal growth is an act of faith followed by action. We must carry the torch, take up the search, and do the work. When we do the work from a position of love, the Universe conspires to help us. As they say at Pine Ridge, "The spirits will meet you halfway."

True love of self is the path we are called to walk. While that path can sometimes seem impossible to locate, the truth is, we are always on it. It's the ultimate irony of a life on Earth: we are often lost, but always home.

As my dear friend Gabrielli LaChiara is fond of saying,

Love is the cure.
You are love.
Therefore, you are the cure.

That's the Seventh Power, and it lives within us all.

＊ ＊ ＊

WHERE MY VOICE GOES FROM HERE is unknown, but I can share with you four promises:

- I will never again say that I have SD.
- I will love and accept the voice I do have as my own.
- I will keep working to make Hancock Lumber a place where everybody leads and the Seventh Power thrives.
- And I will keep blowing bubbles—until the day my free voice returns, or the day my spirit leaves this body.

Many blessings to you! Love and light is the cure, and it resides within us all. We heal the planet by healing ourselves. We are the wound, and we are the cure.

If the Great Spirit had desired me to be a white man he would have made me so in the first place. He put in your heart certain wishes and plans, and in my heart he put other and different desires. Each man is good in His sight. It is not necessary for eagles to be crows.

—SITTING BULL

Online Resources

Best Places to Work in Maine (www.bestplacestoworkinme.com)

Dakota Access Pipeline Facts (daplpipelinefacts.com)

Employee Engagement (news.gallup.com/poll/188144/employee-engagement-stagnant-2015.aspx)

Flag of Planet Earth (www.flagofplanetearth.com)

Hancock Lumber (www.hancocklumber.com)

Holodomor Victims Memorial (memorialholodomor.org.ua/eng)

Jose Miguel Sokoloff, MullenLowe Group (www.mullenlowegroup.com/team/jose-miguel-sokoloff)

Jose Miguel Sokoloff, TED Talk (www.ted.com/talks/jose_miguel_sokoloff_how_christmas_lights_helped_guerrillas_put_down_their_guns)

Kevin Hancock (www.kevindhancock.com)

Map of Human Migration (genographic.nationalgeographic.com/human-journey)

National Spasmodic Dysphonia Association (www.dysphonia.org)

Pine Ridge Indian Reservation Facts (www.re-member.org/pine-ridge-reservation.aspx)

Seeds of Peace (www.seedsofpeace.org)

Singing Horse Trading Post (www.singinghorse.net)

SoulCycle (www.soul-cycle.com)

STAR School (www.starschool.org)

Wind Cave National Park (www.nps.gov/wica/index.htm)

Worldwide Employee Engagement Crisis (news.gallup.com/businessjournal/188033/worldwide-employee-engagement-crisis.aspx)

ZEO Alliance (zeoalliance.com)

Evan Duprey (above left) and the inside cover of the notebook he gave me (above right). As my friend Verola Spider knows, Evan (like all children) is Wakan Yeja, and I am proud to be his friend. The fresh pages of an unused journal are a gift of wonder.

Both the Arizona desert and the Wind Cave National Park in the Black Hills (above) serve as constant reminders that in nature, power is dispersed.

(Above left) Mark Sorenson at his desk at the STAR School on the day we met. (Above right) Waffle House #7004 in Brattleboro, North Carolina. Transparency rules, and everyone leads at Waffle House. (Below) Erin Lindsay, Boston SoulCycle instructor and "girl on fire," on the day I interviewed her at the Parish Café on Boston's Tremont Street.

(Above) The Casco Days midway and (Left) our daughter, Sydney, dressed up as the Hancock Lumber mascot, "Forest," for the Grand Parade.

Tim Wilson, surrounded by Seeds at the camp he helped create in Otisfield, Maine. His parents, Henry and Mamie Wilson—who moved from South Carolina to Pittsburgh in 1921—would be proud. We never know what ripples of goodness our lives might one day help to generate.

The 2017 Seeds of Peace "Paradigm Shifters" on the front porch of the Trophy Room at the camp.

This bronze statue, titled Bitter Memory of Childhood, stands in the center of the walkway at the Holodomor Victims Memorial in Kiev. Overreaching has consequences.

(Top) Hanna Soroka and I share a laugh at the conclusion of our visit in her Soviet-era apartment on the outskirsts of Kiev. (Left) Mykola Onyshchanko and I, on the day we met at the Holodomor Victims Memorial.

Jose Miguel Sokoloff and I at Cecconi's Mayfair Restaurant in London. (You can see Evan's notebook on the table.) Jose envisions a world where everyone feels at home, right where they are.

(Below) The Ringling Bros.
elephant on my bookshelf.
A strength in one generation
can be a weakness in
another, a lesson our
daughter, Sydney (right),
reminded me of with her
Christmas present and note.

Visiting with Verola Spider (left) and Catherine Grey Day (right) at the Singing Horse Trading Post on the Pine Ridge Indian Reservation. "Staying in your lane" is poor advice. Mitakuye Oyasin *(We are all related.)*

Tribal Ordinance 88.01 welcomes visitors to the Pine Ridge Indian Reservation as they approach from Whiteclay, Nebraska.

On the Pine Ridge Indian Reservation near Cuny Table.

About the Author

KEVIN HANCOCK IS THE PRESIDENT of Hancock Lumber Company. Established in 1848, Hancock Lumber operates retail stores, sawmills, and a truss plant led by 525 employees. The company also grows trees on its timberlands in Southern Maine.

Hancock Lumber is a six-time recipient of the Best Places to Work in Maine Award. The company is also a past recipient of the Maine Family Business of the Year Award, the Governor's Award for Business Excellence, the MITC Exporter of the Year Award, and the Pro-Sales National Dealer of the Year Award.

Kevin is a past chairman of the National Lumber and Building Material Dealers Association, as well as the Bridgton Academy

Board of Trustees. He is a recipient of the Ed Muskie Access to Justice Award, the Habitat for Humanity Spirit of Humanity Award, the Boy Scouts of America Distinguished Citizen Award, and *Timber Processing* magazine's Person of the Year Award. Kevin is also a former history teacher and a lifetime youth basketball coach.

Kevin is a graduate of Lake Region High School and Bowdoin College. A frequent visitor to Pine Ridge Indian Reservation in South Dakota, Kevin published his first book about his experiences with the Oglala Sioux Tribe in 2015. Titled *Not for Sale: Finding Center in the Land of Crazy Horse*, the book was featured in *The New York Times* and won the 2015 National Indie Excellence Award, the 2016 Independent Authors Network Award, and the 2016 New York Book Festival Award.

Kevin is an advocate of strengthening the voices of all individuals through listening, empowering, and sharing leadership. Kevin and his wife of thirty years, Alison, have two adult children, Abby and Sydney.

Not For Sale

Finding Center in the Land of Crazy Horse

Written and Photographed by Kevin Hancock

What readers are saying about Kevin Hancock's first book,

Not for Sale: Finding Center in the Land of Crazy Horse

- *"I have read very few books that surprise me. This book is magical. This book is inspiring. This book is timeless."*

- *"I just can't find the words to describe how touched I was by your book."*

- *"Your book came to me for a reason, and just at the right time. I read it twice, and its pages are dotted with my tears (literally)."*

- *"I was totally mesmerized by your gift for weaving your story together so beautifully! Cheers to you for being a listener of whispers, and being brave enough to share your experiences with us all."*

- *"From the time I opened your book it was hard to put it down; it is truly amazing. Thank you for sharing your story!"*

- *"I just finished your book at 3:30 a.m., because I couldn't put it down. I was sorry that there were no more pages to turn. Thank you!"*

- *"Kevin, I just finished your book and need to tell you how much I was moved by it (and often to tears), on so many levels."*

- *"Kevin, thank you for writing this book. Your story touched me, heart and soul."*
- *"I laughed, I cried, and I was inspired by your passion."*
- *"This book is personal, authentic, and written with great style."*
- *"I am savoring your book, enjoying every word. I do not want it to end."*
- *"I feel that I am more aware of my own inner self through your descriptive writing."*
- *"I simply loved this book from start to finish."*

"I read Not for Sale: Finding Center in the Land of Crazy Horse *in record time. I simply could not put this book down. It is my hope that all leaders will heed the message that it is possible to care for our souls and our organizations simultaneously. In fact, for true sustainability and health, we must."*

—CHRISTIANE NORTHRUP, MD, *New York Times* bestselling author
of *Goddesses Never Age*

"Kevin tells his amazing story here: part history, part spiritual journey, part moving portrait of some extraordinary people, and part leadership manual, this fascinating book will touch you and teach you on many levels."

—ANGUS KING, U.S. Senator (I-ME)

attendees were moved by his story, inspired by his work, and drawn to his genuine and loving presence. Every event and gathering would benefit from Kevin's involvement and perspective."

—Graham Pansing Brooks, Director, Do More Good Conference

For more information, contact Kevin's team at:

www.kevindhancock.com | khancock@hancocklumber.com
*"There is a great deal of power to be tapped in creating
an organization where everybody leads…
where everybody makes decisions…
where everybody's empowered."*

-KEVIN HANCOCK

Index